1. Introduction

The 'Liliput' kleinster geländegängiger Kettenschlepper (smallest cross-country tracked towing vehicle), renamed leichter Zugkraftwagen 1t (Sd.Kfz.10) on 17 March 1937, was developed to fill a need for an ultra-light towing vehicle with exceptional terrain-crossing capability coupled with a capability for high road speeds. This was the sixth semi-tracked towing vehicle in the series developed under the guidance of Dipl.Ing. Kniepkamp of Wa Prüf 6 (Army Ordnance Developments Department).

Wa Prüf 6 selected Demag as the detailed design firm and provided guidance in the form of technical specifications which described the performance characteristics and chosen components. New features for this ultra-light Zugkraftwagen were a Wanne (hull) in which all the automotive components were mounted (instead of the traditional frame) and a torsion bar suspension (including the front wheels).

Demag designed and assembled several Versuchs-Fahrzeuge (trial vehicles) series from 1934 to 1936:

- D ll 1 (Demag Lilliput Model 1)
- D ll 2 (Demag Lilliput Model 2)
- D ll 3 (Demag Lilliput Model 3)

Each type was evaluated by Wa Prüf 6. These trials were followed by a Wa Prüf 6 contract for a Versuchs-Serie of eight D 6 (for testing and troop trials) and then a Waffenamt follow-on contract for 60 0-Serie D 6 in 1937, prior to contracts from Wa J Rü for mass production of the final model, the D 7.

In addition to the basic leichter Zugkraftwagen 1to (Sd.Kfz.10), intended to be used for towing light artillery pieces and ammunition trailers, the D 7 Fahrgestell (and, experimentally the predecessor D ll 3 and D 6) was used as the chassis for several variants, including the Gasspürerkraftwagen (Sd.Kfz.10/1) (gas detection vehicle), leichter Entgiftungskraftwagen (Sd. Kfz.10/2) D 7s (decontamination vehicle), leichter Sprühkraftwagen (Sd.Kfz.10/3) D 7k (poison gas spraying vehicle), Selbstfahrlafette (Sd.Kfz.10/4) f. 2cm Flak 30 (self-propelled 20mm anti-aircraft gun), and Selbstfahrlafette (Sd. Kfz.10/5) für 2cm Flak 38.

A related variant, the D 7p Fahrgestell (a shortened version of the D 7 chassis with an armour hull) was used as the chassis for the leichter Schützenpanzerwagen (light armoured personnel carrier) (Sd.Kfz.250) (refer to Panzer Tracts No.15-

1), the leichter ge[...] ight armoured ammun[...] [...]hter gepanzerter Beobachtungskraftwagen (light armoured observation vehicle) (Sd.Kfz.253).

Unfortunately, Wa J Rü decided to only report the major types of vehicles produced as a total sum - not broken down by manufacturer or sub-variant. Wa J Rü reported the total number of le.Zgkw.1t produced each month - but did not systematically include all the D 7 Fahrgestell (chassis) produced for the Nebeltruppe (literally 'fog' or smoke branch, the term coined to disguise its actual intended use as chemical-warfare elements), Truppenluftschutz (anti-aircraft defence), or Nachrictungs-Truppen (signals). During the period from 1938 to March 1942, the D 7 Fahrgestell produced for variants were sometimes included in the monthly production reports as le.Zgkw.1t and sometimes not. And, for part of 1940 and 1941, there was some double reporting of both the D 7p Fahrgestell and the completed armoured vehicles. Due to the simplified method of consolidated reporting by Wa J Rü, an accurate record of how many D 7 Fahrgestell and sub-variants were produced has not survived for the period from 1938 to March 1942, but thanks to Sonderausschuss (special committee) reports an accurate record is available from April 1942 to February 1945.

Hundreds of hours were spent accurately measuring surviving le.Zgkw.1t (Sd.Kfz.10) variants and components in both public museums and private collections. The payoff is the as-built drawings that accurately represent the le.Zgkw.1t (Sd.Kfz.10) and variants as they were actually produced.

As is our high standard, Panzer Tracts are based solely on surviving specimens, wartime photographs, and the content of primary source documents written by those who participated in the design, production, and employment of the Zugkraftwagen. The time is long overdue for those real experts who designed, produced, and used the le.Zgkw.1t (Sd.Kfz.10) to have their say.

Note: Weight designation. In original German documents the method of designating the weight varies between 1 to and 1t depending on the writer and period, both signifying 1 metric ton. For ease of reading, Panzer Tracts has chosen to only use 1t as this was in the title of all the D-Vorschriften (maintenance manuals).

2. Development

Despite searching for close to 40 years in archives and museums around the world, we have not found the original documents written by those responsible for design development of the 'Lilliput'. However, directly after the war, British military intelligence obtained original documents and interviewed personnel from Demag which they used to create a 'secondary' source document - the *BAOR Technical Intelligence Report No.81 dated 29 June 1946 on the German Semi-Tracked Vehicle Development from 1934 Onwards*. Their version of the development history is related in the following excerpts:

The first model, LL 1 (1934-5) was considerably smaller than the later types. The chassis was of hull construction, with high sides, and the 6-cylinder BMW engine was mounted in the rear, leaving practically no loading space. The driving sprocket was at the front, and had plain central driving teeth, instead of the roller type used in the later models. There were only 3 interleaved rubber-tyred roadwheels per side, one narrowly and

two widely spaced. The track links were provided with two flat guide-horns, which passed on either side of the narrowly spaced roadwheels, and not between the two halves as with later types. Photographs show two types of track, one having needle-bearings and rubber track pads, the other with plain bar-shaped steel spuds.

The front axle arrangements were of an unusual character. A tubular axle, pivoted in the centreline of the vehicle so as to have a limited swinging movement in a plane at right angles, carried trailing parallel links at either end, the other ends of the links carrying the front wheel steering knuckles and ball-joints. The top link on either side was sprung with a short torsion bar which was enclosed in the tubular axle and anchored at the centre. Shock absorbers and snubber blocks were provided to limit the swinging of the front axle, which was not itself provided with any form of springing.

The next model, LL 2 (1935) was almost identical in its

A D ll 1 (Demag Liliput Model 1) photographed in 1935 with a torsion bar suspension for the front wheels and also torsion bar suspension for the three roadwheels. (NARA)

general features with the LL 1, except that it has four road wheels per side, the length of the tracked portion being somewhat increased. Both these models were purely experimental.

With the LL 3 (1936), the vehicle began to take on its final shape. The engine, a 42 horsepower 6-cylinder BMW, was mounted in the front. The front axle suspension used in the earlier models was retained (but without any shock absorbers). A divided track-rod, with an intermediate lever, as used in some of the Adler experimental vehicles, was used for front-wheel steering. The number of road wheels used in the tracked suspension, which was sprung, as throughout the series, by torsion bars, was increased to 5 per side. All three models described so far had torsion bar springing for the idlers. Some specimens of the LL 3 had solid rubber front tyres and all-steel tracks, others had pneumatic front tyres and rubber-padded tracks. In this model the driving sprocket was provided with roller-teeth. A total of 38 was produced.

The next model to be designed was the D 4. This remained purely a drawing board vehicle, no specimen being constructed. There was no model designated D 5.

The D 6, constructed in 1937-38, was virtually the same as the D 7, which was the standard production model through the war. The D 6 used an 83 horsepower 6-cylinder Maybach NL 38 engine, as did some early specimens of the D 7, the later ones having a 100 horsepower Maybach HL 42. It also had a six-speed Demag-Adler transmission, as against a seven-speed vacuum-operated preselective Maybach Variorex in the D 7. Apart from minor differences in dimensions, constructional features of both these models were very similar, both chassis being of hull construction. The front axle was a normal beam type, sprung by a transverse semi-elliptic leaf spring. The driving sprockets had roller teeth. There were five interleaved, torsion bar sprung road wheels per side; the idlers were not sprung, but were provided with shear-bolt safety devices. Sixty specimens of the D 6 were produced.

While there are factual elements in technical intelligence reports, there are also mistakes. In part these mistakes are due to attempting to reconstruct pre-war history by interviewing personnel long after the events occurred without the interviewed personnel having access to period documents. However, the Allies' military intelligence was not alone in making mistakes. In several cases, the Heeres-Waffenamt (Army Weapons Agency) created false impressions in their one-page data sheets by mixing photos of trial pieces in with data from later models. This is the case with the data sheet on the Demag D ll 2 where the photos shown on the page were of its predecessor the Demag D ll 1.

This original data sheet from 1935/36 recorded that the

Kleinster geländegängiger Kettenschlepper Bauart D ll 2 1935 (Demag Liliput 2 model 1935) was built by Demag A.G., Duisberg. Weighing 2.5 metric tons, its normal towing capacity was 600 kg. With a 30 metric horsepower engine, the maximum speed was 50 km/hr, the range on roads was 250 km, and it could climb a grade of 24° without a load, reduced to 12° with a load. It was intended for towing a 3.7cm Tak (Tankabwehr-Kanone) (anti-tank gun) and a leichter Munitions-Anhänger (light ammunition trailer).

As mentioned in the BAOR Technical Intelligence Report, the D ll 3 had five interleaved rubber-tyred roadwheels, the disk of which had six holes to reduce the weight. The inner wheels and the idler had even larger holes. The idler wheel was set closer to the ground. The outer tyre diameter of the roadwheels used on a D ll 3 was 530mm. As a result of the longer track, a crew of six could now be transported. Initial trials were with solid steel track links. Further development saw the introduction of rubber padded track. The wheel disks were also strengthened by the addition of a star pattern pressing.

The postwar claim that a total of 38 D ll 3 were produced is not confirmed by original inventory reports. The entire inventory reported by the Luftwaffe on 1 January 1938 was two Zgkw.1t (Sd.Kfz.10). The O.K.H./A.H.A. reported that it had zero Zgkw.1t on hand on 1 April 1938. These inventory reports did not include trial series vehicles paid for by Wa Prüf 6, but a Versuchs-Serie was normally limited from two to five vehicles - not 38.

Eight Versuchs-Serie D 6 were produced by Demag before the run of 60 production 0-Serie. These Versuchs-Serie D 6 had 6-cylinder Maybach NL 38 TRK engines rated at 90 horsepower at 2800 rpm and a leaf-spring suspension for the front axle. The Laufwerk (running gear) was redesigned, the five interleaved rubber tyred roadwheels being reduced in diameter to 500mm and fabricated in such a way as to be lighter but stronger. The idler wheel remained the same diameter as the D ll 3 but was also redesigned. The Versuchs-Serie D 6 still had a similar body to its predecessor, the D ll 3, with some detailed changes ahead of the front axle and additional air vents in the Kotflügel (fender).

The post-war technical intelligence report is also incorrect in several details about the D 6, including the type of transmission installed. On 7 July 1937, Maybach reported on the status of its transmission work, as follows:

Transmission SRG 102128 (Motor NL 38) - 7 speeds forward for the Lilliput Typ 'D 6'. Eight are to be delivered this month to Demag. Two transmissions are to go to Adler where unpolished gears are to be installed. The Schaltkasten (shifting

A D ll 1 photographed in 1935 towing a 3.7cm Tak (anti-tank gun) and an ammunition trailer. The design of the D ll 1 was directed by Herr Kniepkamp of Wa Prüf 6 and was unique in having a Wanne (hull) to support all the automotive components instead of a frame. (NARA)

Right: The suspension was lengthened on the D ll 2 (Demag Liliput Model 2) with four interleaved roadwheels. It had the same rear mounted 6-cylinder BMW engine rated at 30 metric horsepower as its predecessor, the D ll 1. (TTM)

Below: The D ll 1 was also unique in having the 1.479 litre 6-cylinder BMW gasoline engine rated at 30 metric horsepower mounted at the rear. This D ll 1 is being tested with unlubricated pin cast steel track links with better off-road traction than the lubricated needle-bearing track links with rubber pads. (TTM)

box for this semi-automatic transmission) is mounted separately. Delivery deadline is 15 July 1937

A Waffenamt data sheet listing details about all the Zugkraftwagen types in service in 1940 provides the following data. The D 6 was produced at three assembly plants - Demag, Adler, and Mechanische Werke Cottbus - with a Maybach NL 38 TRK engine rated at 90 metric horsepower. Originally it had 42 Zgw.50/240/150 (cast lubricated needle bearing, 240mm wide, 150mm pitch) track links with Polster-Typ W 100 rubber pads, which were superseded during the production run by Zpw.51/240/160 track links with Polster-Typ W 102 pads (the same type of track links used on the D 7). 6.00-20 Gelände (off-road) pneumatic tyres were mounted on the front wheels.

Engines installed in new vehicle series after 1 October 1938 were to be configured to use OZ 74 (74 octane) gasoline. On 16 May 1940, O.K.H. reported that Maybach engines (NL 38 TRK Motor Nr.50001-50068) had pistons that created compression too high for OZ 74 gasoline. A Maybach report lists the NL 38 TRK Motor Nr.50001-50068 as being installed in the first Demag models (D 6). NL 38 TRKM engines with a new cylinder head and shorter pistons were installed starting with Motor Nr.50069 in the Serienausführung (mass produced D 7).

As reported by O.K.H. on 12 May 1937, a total of 107 le.Zgkw. (Sd.Kfz.10) were still to be delivered from current orders. After testing the Versuchs-Fahrzeuge (trial vehicles), plans were to order 8235 le.Zgkw. in June 1937. An overview of procurement for the Luftwaffe dated 30 September 1937 included six l.Zgkw.1t (Sd.Kfz. 10) to be delivered in March 1938. O.K.H. /A.H.A. reported that no Zgkw.1t were on hand on 1 April 1938, 11 were delivered from 1 April to 30 June 1938, and 22 arrived from 1 July to 30 September 1938. The first monthly report from Wa J Rü dated February 1939 recorded that 60 Zgkw.1t had been completed in January 1939 and 5 the previous month. A total of 81 were reported as completed between April and December 1938. Therefore, the 68 D 6 (including 8 Versuch-Serie and 60 0-Serie) were completed by November 1938.

Automotive Data for 1-ton Zugkraftwagen (BAOR Tech Intel Report No.81)

Model	LL 1	LL 2	LL 3	D 4	D 6
Engine	BMW 28 HP/2800 rpm	BMW 28 HP/2800 rpm	BMW 42 HP/2800 rpm	Maybach 65 HP/3000 rpm	Maybach NL 38 83 HP/2400 rpm
Transmission	ZF 4 speed	ZF 4 speed	ZF 4 speed	ZF 4 speed	Demag-Adler 6 speed
Front Wheel Suspension	Torsion Bar	Torsion Bar	Torsion Bar	Transverse Leaf Spring	Transverse Leaf Spring
Tracked Suspension	3 Roadwheels Torsion Bar	4 Roadwheels Torsion Bar	5 Roadwheels Torsion Bar	5 Roadwheels Torsion Bar	5 Roadwheels Torsion Bar
Laden Weight		2560 kg	3400 kg	3750 kg	3850 kg
Towed Load		600 kg	600 kg	600 kg	600 kg
Overall Length		3.40m	4.40m	4.75m	4.721m
Overall Width		1.60m	1.80m	1.90m	1.824m
Overall Height		1.70m	1.70m	1.75m	1.75m

Opposite: A D ll 3 being demonstrated towing a 2cm Flak (anti-aircraft gun), 3.7cm Pak (anti-tank gun), and a 7.5cm le.I.G. (infantry gun). The large idler wheel with torsion bar suspension also served as a sixth roadwheel for improved flotation on soft ground. A D ll 3 was also used to create a trial 2cm Flak Selbstfahrlafette (self-propelled carriage). (NARA)

Opposite bottom: A metre longer than its predecessor, the D ll 3 could seat a crew of five or six. (TTM)

Above: The D ll 3 had a larger 1.971 litre 6-cylinder BMW petrol engine rated at 30 metric horsepower conventionally mounted in front for improved cooling and five interleaved flat-disc roadwheels with torsion bar suspension. It still retained torsion bar suspension for the front wheels. (NARA)

Below: Demag produced eight Versuchs-Serie D 6 vehicles in its trial series, featuring a leaf-spring suspension for the front axle, a Maybach NL 38TRM 90 PS engine, and 500mm diameter roadwheels. This example includes several unique features, such as the shape of the fenders, the addition of louvres (instead of wire mesh) in the side ventilation ports, the use of a new tyre pattern, and 42 track links per side, each with a longer pitch and a rubber pad. (HLD)

Above: One of 60 production 0-Serie D 6 Fahrgestell with large, screened openings on the engine cover sides, a rounded fender over the front wheels, a large engine air intake filter mounted externally on the right side, 6.00-20 (off-road) tyres, and 42 Zgw.50/240/150 rubber padded track links per side. (TTM)

Below: This production 0-Serie D 6 has the same style Aufbau (superstructure) that was adopted as standard on the le.Zgkw.1t (Sd. Kfz.10) Typ D 7 with driver's side doors opened by sliding them down. During the production 0-Serie D 6 run, the Zgw.50/240/150 cast track links with lubricated needle-bearing track and rubber pads were superseded by Zpw.51/240/160 forged track links with a longer pitch, the same type mounted on the D 7. (TA)

Le. Munitionskraftwagen and le.Beobachtungskraftwagen (based on the D 7p) that were intended to support assault-gun batteries of the artillery's 3rd Training Regiment (Artillerie-Lehr-Regiment 3), field expedient versions were created. Production D 6's were used for this purpose. This photo shows a conversion to an observation vehicle. (KHM & AMC)

3. Improvements to Create the D 7

As shown by the following drawing numbers from the Ersatzteilliste (replacement parts list) D672/4 (dated 5 September 1941), new components designed specifically for the D 7 are identified by the Gruppen Nr. (standardised WaA drawing numbers) 021 Gr 26851 to 26874. Components inherited from the Versuchs-Serie D 6 (two generations back) are identified with Demag drawing numbers RS 2100 to RS 3052. Only a few components had been designed for its immediate predecessor, the 0-Serie D 6, identified by Gruppen Nr. 021 Gr 26501 to 26550.

NL 38 TRKM	**Maybach-Motor** (Maybach engine)	
021 B 26851	**Motorbefestigung** (engine mount)	
021 B 26852	**Gelenkwelle** (drive shaft)	
SRG 102 128	**Schaltgetriebe** (transmission)	
RS 2100	**Lenkgetriebe** (steering unit)	
RS 2128	**Kettenantrieb** (track drive)	
021 B 26854/5	**Triebrad, links u. rechts** (drive sprocket)	
021 B 26860	**Wanne** (hull)	
RS 2883	**Vorderachse** (front axle)	
RS 2199	**Blattfeder** (leaf spring)	
021 B 26506	**Laufradschwinge** (swing arms)	
RS 2298	**Äußeres Laufrad** (outer roadwheel)	
RS 2192	**Inneres Laufrad** (inner roadwheel)	
021 B 26856	**Drehstabfeder** (torsion bars)	
021 B 26508	**Leitradschwinge** (idler arm)	
021 B 26863	**Lenkung** (steering)	

021 B 26866	**Kühler** (radiator)	
021 B 26867U1	**Kotflügel** (fender)	
RS 3052	**Lampenhalter** (light holder)	
021 B 26867U5	**Kettenkotblech** (track guard)	
021 B 26867U8	**Schutzblech für Auspuff** (heat guard)	
021 B 26867U10	**Stirnwandverkleidung** (radiator cover)	
021 B 26867U11	**Motorhaube** (engine cover)	
021 B 26867U30	**Verkleidung mit Luftkanal** (cover with ventilation channel)	
021 B 26867U32	**Werkzeugkasten** (tool box)	
021 B 26869U1	**Brennstoffbehälter, links** (fuel tank, L)	
021 B 26869U2	**Brennstoffbehälter, rechts** (fuel tank, R)	
021 B 26870	**Abgasschalldämpfer** (exhaust muffler)	
RS 2229	**Anhängerkupplung** (tow pintle)	
021 B 26874	**Sitz** (seat)	
021 B 33331	**Kettenglied Zpw.51/240/160** (track link)	
021 B 36540	**Metallaufbau mit Klappverdeck** (upper body with convertible top)	

The D 7 had 41 track links with 160mm pitch compared to the 42 track links with 150mm pitch on the D 6. The front wheels had 6.00-20 (Luka) tyres compared to 6.00-20 gel. (off-road) tyres for the D 6. Configured as a le.Zgkw.1t (Sd.Kfz.10), most Typ D 7 were completed with a low profile upper body with sliding side doors, although at the start of production some were completed with an upper body with hinged side doors.

This production 0-Serie D 6 has a large cylindrical silencer for the engine exhaust mounted on the left side (others still had the exhaust pipe extended out the rear). An idler wheel (larger in diameter than the roadwheels) was mounted in a raised position without a torsion bar suspension. The Aufbau (upper body) was specially developed for Nachrichtung (Signals) units. It had higher sides, a covered load area and hinged doors for the driver's and co-driver. A small number of these Nachrichtung vehicles were also built on the production D 7 chassis. (TA)

4. Description

The description and operating instructions for the D 7 Fahrgestell (chassis) for the leichter Zugkraftwagen (Sd. Kfz.10) are contained in manual D672/3 dated 1 March 1939.

The leichter Zugkraftwagen (Sd.Kfz.10) is a half-track vehicle with front wheels and tracked suspension. The chassis, model Zgkw.1t Typ D 7, is steered by the front wheels and both tracks. Instead of a frame, all automotive components are mounted in/on a Wanne (hull) made out of carbon steel.

Power is provided by a 6-cylinder 3.791 litre Maybach NL 38 TRKM gasoline engine (rated at 90 metric horsepower at 2800 rpm) with a 130-Watt Lichtmaschine (electrical generator) driven by a fan belt.

The semi-automatic Maybach VG 102 128 Schaltregler-Getriebe (transmission) has seven forward and three reverse speeds. The desired gear selected with a short hand lever. Shifting initiated by disengaging the clutch, is done automatically by a vacuum system. The maximum speed of 65 km/hr is achieved in seventh gear at an engine speed of 2400 rpm. The speeds of the other six forward (and three reverse) gears are based on an engine speed of 2800 rpm. Therefore, the highest speed that could be achieved in seventh gear was actually 76 km/hr, but the driver was warned not to exceed 65 km/hr.

When steering with the steering wheel, only the front wheels are turned initially, so that shallow curves are negotiated the same as a normal wheeled vehicle, with the Lenkgetriebe (steering unit) acting as a normal compensating differential. When the steering wheel is turned farther, linkage and hydraulic cylinders connected to the Lenkbremse (steering brakes) cause the steering brakes on the right or left side to be applied. The further the steering wheel is turned, the more the steering brake is applied so that sharper curves can be negotiated.

The Triebrad (drive wheel with 12 rollers instead of teeth) is attached to the final drive, which is driven by the steering unit.

The suspension consists of five Laufräder (double roadwheels) with solid rubber tyres per side mounted on swing arms each with a torsion bar. There are no shock absorbers mounted in the hull to dampen the torsion bars. The only dampening of any vehicle oscillation is by a pair of Boge Stossdämpfer (shock absorbers) mounted at the front axle.

A Leitrad (idler wheel), mounted on a swing arm on each

One of the first le.Zgkw.1t (Sd.Kfz.10) with a D 7 chassis assembled at Adlerwerke was sent to Maybach in Friedrichshafen for testing. The running gear wheels on a D 7 were enlarged to 550mm diameter. The vehicle in the background is an O-Serie VK 901, the description of which can be found in Panzer Tracts No.2-2. (MA)

side, is used to adjust the track tension. If there is too much stress on the tracks, an Abscherbolzen (shear pin) retaining the adjusting bolt will break, relieving the track tension.

The Gleisketten (track) held together by Bolzen (track pins) have 41 Zpw.51/240/160 (or Kgw.51/240/160) Kettenglieder (track links) with Polster Typ W 102 (rubber pads) on both sides. The rubber pads are bolted are bolted onto the track links for higher road speeds. To reduce rolling resistance, each track link has lubricated needle bearings.

The Aufbau (upper body) is made up of the track guards on the sides, the rigid rear walls, and the sliding Einstiegklappen (side doors). The angled fenders at the rear of the track guards can be folded up for removing or installing the tracks.

The Gepäckbrücke (baggage bin) behind the Fahrer- und Beifahrersitz (driver's and co-driver's seats) separates the inner Aufbau into a forward and rear compartment and binds both track guards together. These compartments are accessible through the side doors that can be lowered, which also serve as a back rest and arm rest for the crew.

There are two Sitzkasten (seat bins) covered with cushions,

each for three men in the rear compartment aligned along the sides. The lids are opened toward the interior of the vehicle to allow easier loading into the Sitzkasten with the Einstiegklappen lowered.

Two hatches in the middle of the floor allow access to the space below for storing vehicle accessories: the anti-skid snow chains, tow cable, and S-Haken (S hooks).

The windscreen is removable, with a distance of 1400mm between the mounting pins.

The Klappverdeck (convertible top) is mounted at the rear of the rigid side walls and at the front on the windscreen. Reinforced camouflaged Segeltuch (sail canvas) is used for the cover. A tent window is located in the rear. Four side pieces, each with a window, are secured to the wooden frame and the Aufbau. The canvas top can be folded together to the rear and secured by two rests.

A Werkzeugkasten (tool box) is mounted behind the right fender.

One of the first le.Zgkw.1t (Sd.Kfz.10) with a D 7 chassis completed by Büssing-NAG in 1939. This has the two-tone (RAL 46 Dunkelgrau and RAL 45 Dunkelbraun) camouflage introduced in mid-1937. (NARA)

313.39K

Above: The same le.Zgkw.1t (Sd.Kfz.10) with a D 7 chassis completed by Büssing-NAG as on page 22-1-13 is used to demonstrate the towing of a 2cm Flak 30. (NARA)
Below: Towing a Sonderanhänger 32 (Sd.Ah.32) für Munition (single-axle ammunition trailer). (NARA)

Control panel. 1. *Switch box with starter button.* ***2.*** *Tachometer.* ***3.*** *Steering wheel position indicator.* ***4.*** *Thermometer for cooling water.* ***5.*** *Oil pressure gauge.* ***6.*** *Odometer.* ***7.*** *Red warning lamp for indicator.* ***8.*** *Blue warning lamp for indicator.* ***9.*** *Indicator switch.* ***10.*** *Socket for hand lamp.* ***11.*** *Lever for radiator panel.* ***12.*** *Lever for hand throttle.* ***13.*** *Plunger for central lubrication.* ***14.*** *Fuel tap.* ***15.*** *Hand brake lever.* ***16.*** *Gearbox pre-selector lever.* ***17.*** *Power socket for windshield wipers.* ***18.*** *Switch for instrument panel lighting.* ***19.*** *Sun visor.* ***20.*** *Starter flap.* ***21.*** *Control for air filter.* ***22.*** *Horn.* ***23.*** *Ignition switch.* ***(D672/3)***

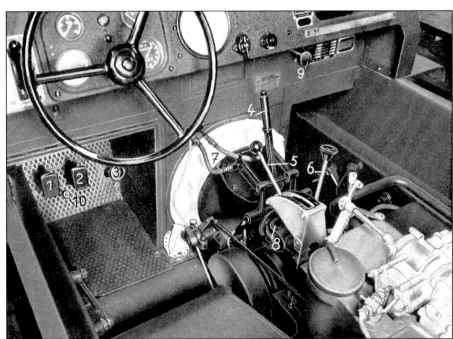

Arrangement of the operating levers. 1. *Clutch pedal.* ***2.*** *Brake pedal.* ***3.*** *Accelerator pedal.* ***4.*** *Handbrake lever.* ***5.*** *Gear preselector lever.* ***6.*** *Shift lever for forward and reverse gear.* ***7.*** *Oil pressure line to the steering brake.* ***8.*** *Cardan joint shaft.* ***9.*** *Plug for central pressure lubrication.* ***10.*** *Dimmer switch.* ***(D672/3)***

5. Production

As reported by O.K.H. on 12 May 1937, after testing the Versuchs-Fahrzeuge (trial vehicles), plans were to order 8235 le.Zgkw. in June 1937. Contracts were awarded to Zahnradfabrik, Friedrichshafen, and Büssing-NAG, Berlin-Oberschöneweide, by July 1937 for 1680 transmissions to be delivered at the rate of 25 per month starting in February 1938 for the 60 0-Serie Typ D 6 followed by the mass production series Typ D 7. Maybach NL 38 TRKM engines were to be available starting on 1 October 1938 for the start of the mass production series Typ D 7.

O.K.H./A.H.A. reported that 11 Zgkw.1t were delivered from 1 April to 30 June 1938, 22 arrived from 1 July to 30 September 1938, and 900 were planned to be completed from 1 October 1938 to 31 March 1939. The start of the mass production of the Typ D 7 was delayed due to continuous modifications.

One of the first leichte Zugmaschine D 7 was demonstrated on the Hainberg, a test ground near Nürnberg, for Oberstleutnant Fichtner (Wa Prüf 6), Regierungs-Baurat Kniepkamp (Wa Prüf 6), and Oberbaurat Esser (Kummersdorf) on 11 October 1938.

The first monthly production report from Wa J Rü dated February 1939 recorded that 60 Zgkw.1t had been completed in January 1939, 5 the previous month, and a total of 81 completed between April and December 1938 (for a total of 60 D 6 and 21 D 7 completed in 1938). The monthly production statistics reported by Wa J Rü are shown in the table on the right.

On 13 April 1939, O.K.H./A.H.A./In 6 announced that the leichter Zugkraftwagen 1t (Sd.Kfz.10) had been tested and accepted as standard army equipment.

On 23 June 1939, A.H.A./In 6 reported the needs of the individual weapons branches for 1t Zgkw. chassis, including 2100 Sd.Kfz.10 for towing 15cm s.I.G. (heavy infantry guns), 4750 for towing anti-tank guns and 72 Sd.Kfz.10/1 for the Nebeltruppe to outfit units that were to be created by 1 October 1942.

On 20 December 1939, the monthly goal for Zgkw.1t was set at 200 per month, of which 30 were to be used for special purposes (five Sd.Kfz.10/1 and 25 Sd.Kfz.10/4) and the rest as normal Zgkw.1t (Sd.Kfz.10).

There were 2502 1t Zgkw. on hand with the Heer and 193 with the Luftwaffe on 1 May 1940, directly before the campaign in the West against France.

On 3 May 1940, plans were made to increase D 7 chassis production from 200 to 300 per month, including 225 Zgkw.1t (Sd.Kfz.10) Ausf.B, 30 Gasspürerkw. (Sd.Kfz.10/1) (gas detection variant), and 45 Sfl. 2cm Flak 30 (Sd.Kfz.10/4) for the Luftwaffe.

In the Heeres Panzerprogramm 1941 (long-term production plans for the next five years) dated 30 May 1941, the Heereswaffenamt (Army Weapons Agency) reported that the Heer needed 5725 Sd.Kfz.10 and 144 Sd.Kfz.10/1.

Details on production from each assembly plant (as reported by the Sonderausschuss) and the totals reported by Wa J Rü from April 1942 to March 1943 are shown in the table below.

le.Zgkw.1t (Sd.Kfz.10) Production as Reported by Wa J Rü based on WaA Abnahme (Waffenamt Acceptance)

Month	1938	1939	1940	1941	1942
January		60	114	259*	175
February		91	235	225*	187
March		154	324	243*	242
April		190	323	194	249
May	11	199	232	225	249
June		149	195	201	240
July		252	206	181	225
August	22	156	223	165	230
September		144	285	224	278
October		219	301	228	224
November	48	110	302	227	254
December		114	235	214	260
Total	81	1838	2975*	2586	2813

* The 1940 total may include 55 D 7p chassis for Sd.Kfz.252/253.
* The Jan-Mar 1941 reports may include 255 D 7p chassis for Sd.Kfz.252/253.

Production of the 1t Zgkw. continued at a high rate of about 250 per month until the Autumn of 1943, when the

Adler assembly plant was diverted to increase m.S.P.W. (Sd. Kfz.251) production and Saurer was diverted to increase 8t Zgkw. and RSO production. This left Mechanische Werke Cottbus (M.W.C.) as the sole assembly plant completing 1t Zgkw. and Sfl. 2cm Flak in 1944. Even M.W.C. production was diverted in 1944 from D 7 to D 7p chassis for the le.S.P.W. (Sd.Kfz.250) (refer to Panzer Tracts No.15-1).

The last of the M.W.C. contracts for D 7 chassis were completed by November 1944, but both M.W.C. and Demag were still producing D 7p chassis. Due to the deteriorating situation toward the end of the war, a Not (Auslauf) Programm (final emergency production program), dated 28 February 1945, called for D 7p Fahrgestell production to cease by May 1945, with M.W.C. scheduled to complete its last 150 in March 1945. Demag was to complete 26 in March and its last 100 in April 1945. Due to a shortage of armour bodies for le.S.P.W. (Sd.Kfz.250), these last 276 D 7p Fahrgestell were to be completed as Zugkraftwagen (towing vehicles) with Pritschen-Aufbau (wooden flat beds). On 1 March 1945, Wa A/WuG6 reported that 80 had been delivered directly to the troops as towing vehicles, with plans to complete another 176 in March and 100 in April 1945.

5.1 Fahrgestell (Chassis) Production

In addition to the design firm of Demag, Wetter/Ruhr (code ccd), the D 7 Fahrgestell was completed under licence at six additional assembly firms: Adlerwerke, Frankfurt a.M. (code arh), Büssing NAG, Berlin (code kan), Mechanische Werke Cottbus (code jfq), M.I.A.G., Braunschweig (code bal), M.N.H., Hannover (code csh), and Saurerwerke, Wien (code ngb). Demag, Adlerwerke, and Büssing-NAG, already in production in 1938, were joined by M.W.C., M.I.A.G., and M.N.H. in early 1939, and Saurerwerke by 1 April 1940.

5.1.1 Demag AG, Wetter/Ruhr (Chassis Number Series 100001)

Initially, Demag was awarded contracts to complete 738 D 7 chassis with Fgst.Nr.100001 to 100738. Then 100 chassis numbers Fgst.Nr.100739 to 100838 were assigned to D 7p chassis for the le.gep.Beob.Kw. (Sd.Kfz.253), and le.gep.Mun. Trsp.Kw. (Sd.Kfz.252). The next 200 Fgst.Nr.(100839 to 101038) were assigned to D 7 chassis for le.Zgkw. (Sd.Kfz.10). Demag continued the D 7p production with Fgst.Nr.101039 to about 102100 with these chassis being used for le.gep.Beob. Kw. (Sd.Kfz.253) le.gep.Mun.Trsp.Kw. (Sd.Kfz.252), and the mass production series le.S.P.W. (Sd.Kfz.250).

An additional series of about 500 Fgst.Nr. (from about 102101 to 102600) were reserved for D 7 chassis for the le.Zgkw. (Sd.Kfz.10), but these were not all used, and Demag

continued D 7p chassis for le.S.P.W. (Sd.Kfz.250) from about Fgst.Nr.102601.

Altogether, Demag completed about 1075 D 7 Fahrgestell from 1938 to November 1942 in the Fgst.Nr. Serie from 100001 to 102600.

5.1.2 Adlerwerke (Fgst.Nr.Serie 200001)

Adlerwerke did not reserve a separate series of Fgst.Nr. for D 7 chassis numbers but mixed them together with their numbers for the D 7p chassis. Having started production in 1938, Adlerwerke reported completion of 1693 D 7 mit normal Aufbau, 736 D 7 mit Sfl. Flak Aufbau, and 273 vehicles with the D 7p Fahrgestell by 31 December 1941. In the following year, the numbers were 2005, 1009 and 650, respectively.

Altogether, Adlerwerke completed 3414 D 7 Fahrgestell by the end of December 1943 in Fgst.Nr. Serie from 200001 to about 205364.

5.1.3 Büssing-NAG, Berlin (Fgst.Nr.Serie 300001)

The third assembly plant, Büssing-NAG, Berlin-Oberschöneweide, used a separate Fgst.Nr. series starting with 300001 for their D 7 chassis. Based on chassis analysis, Büssing-NAG had completed about 650 D 7 chassis by the end of 1941. They completed the last 50 D 7 chassis between April and December 1942, when Büssing dropped out of D 7 production. Altogether, Büssing-NAG completed about 750 D 7 chassis from 1938 to December 1942 in Fgst.Nr. series from 300001 to about 300750.

5.1.4 Mechanische Werke Cottbus (Fgst.Nr.Serie 400001)

Mechanische Werke Cottbus GmbH, Cottbus, was the fourth assembly plant to be awarded contracts for assembling D 7 chassis. Based on chassis number analysis, M.W.C. completed about 200 by the end of 1939 and another 1700 by the end of 1941. They completed 650 D 7 chassis during the period from April to November 1942, another 1255 in 1943, and 536 from January to May 1944.

After Adler and Saurer dropped out in October/December 1943, M.W.C. was left as the sole assembly plant for D 7 chassis. M.W.C. was awarded contract 213-0025/41H to produce 500 le.Zgkw. of which 75 were to be completed as Sd.Kfz.10/5 and 425 as Sd.Kfz.10. All 75 Sd.Kfz.10/5 and 234 Sd.Kfz.10 from this contract had been completed by the end of 1943. This left 191 Sd.Kfz.10 to be completed from January to November 1944, as shown in the table on the next page.

M.W.C. Production in 1944

	le.Zgkw. (Sd.Kfz.10) Contract 213-0025/41		Sfl. (Sd.Kfz.10/5) Contract 213-0013/41	
	Accepted	**Running Total**	**Accepted**	**Running Total**
Jan	91	325	25	225
Feb	10	335	60	285
Mar	10	345	140	425
Apr	20	365	50	475
May	0	365	130	605
Jun	0	365	115	720
Jul	25	390	30	750
Aug	0	390	25	775
Sep	0	390	25	800
Oct	25	415	2	802
Nov	10	425	85+13	900
Dec	Contract completed		Contract completed	

M.W.C. was also awarded contract 213-0029/41H for 900 le.Zgkw. to be completed as Sd.Kfz.10/5. A total of 200 from this contract had been completed by the end of 1943, leaving 700 to be completed from January to November 1944 as shown in the accompanying table. As ordered in October 1944, 13 out of the contract for 900 Sd.Kfz. 10/5 were completed as le.Zgkw. (Sd.Kfz.10) in November 1944. Altogether M.W.C. completed about 4750 D 7 chassis in Fgst.Nr. Serie from 400001 to about 404750 from 1939 to November 1944.

5.1.5 Mühlenbau-Industrie A.G. (M.I.A.G.), Braunschweig (Fgst.Nr.Serie 500001)

The fifth assembly firm, M.I.A.G., started D 7 chassis assembly in late 1939/early 1940. M.I.A.G. completed about 324 D 7 chassis in Fgst.Nr. Serie 500001 to 500324 from 1939 to 1941.

5.1.6 Maschinenfabrik Niedersachsen Hannover (M.N.H.) (Fgst.Nr.Serie 600001)

The sixth assembly plant to be awarded contracts for D 7

The first 641 le.Zgkw.1t (Sd.Kfz.10) with D 7 chassis, completed by Büssing-NAG up to Fgst.Nr.300641 from 1938 to 1940, had a different Wanne 247509 (sheet metal hull) and initial Äußere Laufräder RS 2298 (outer roadwheel) and Innere Laufräder RS 2192 (inner roadwheel). (CM)

chassis assembly, M.N.H., completed about 600 D 7 chassis in Fgst.Nr. Serie 600001 to 600600 from 1939 to November 1942.

5.1.7 Saurerwerke, Wien (Fgst.Nr.Serie 700001)

The last assembly firm, Österreichische Saurerwerke in Wien, Austria did not get started with D 7 chassis production until 1940. It completed about 200 in 1940, 700 in 1941, 1000 in 1942, and 1074 in 1943 for a total of about 3075 D 7 chassis in Fgst.Nr. Serie 700001 to 703075.

5.2 Component Production

5.2.1 Maybach NL 38 TRKM/HL 42 TRKM Engines

In addition to Maybach (code cre), the designer of the engines, three other assembly plants Nordbau (code nct), Auto Union (code hul), and Adlerwerke (code arh) completed NL 38/HL 42 engines under licence.

Maybach used Motor Nr.50069 to 53100 for the NL 38 TRKM and Motor Nr. starting with 53101 for HL 42 TRKM; both types were used solely in Typ D 7 Fahrgestell. For example, Motor Nr.58963 was installed in Fgst.Nr.701602, a le.Zgkw.1t (Sd.Kfz.10) completed by Saurerwerke in 1942.

Nordbau produced 511 NL 38/HL 42 in fiscal year (1 April - 31 March) 1938/39, 1047 in 1939/40, 2199 in 1940/41, 2827 in 1941/42, 3250 in 1942/43, and 449 in 1943/44. Nordbau completed their last 28 HL 42 TRKM for D 7 chassis in May 1943. Nordbau used Motor Nr. starting with 550001 for their NL38/HL 42 TRKM. For example, Motor Nr.553330 was installed in Fgst.Nr.203549, a le.Zgkw.1t (Sd.Kfz.10) completed by Adlerwerke in 1942.

Adlerwerke started production of HL 42 engines in January 1942, completing 2031 in 1942, 6150 in 1943, 6378 in 1944, and 655 from January to March 1945. Only about 15% of these were HL 42 TRKM for the Zgkw.1t, with most being completed as HL 42 TRKM-P for the D 7p chassis, HL 42 TUKRM for HKL6 chassis, and HL 42 TUKRRM for HKL6p chassis. Adlerwerke used Motor-Nr.-Serie starting with 300001 for their HL 42 TRKM, and on 1 September 1943, switched to a new numbering system. Namely, Motor Nr.2 arh 2241. For example, Motor Nr.2 arh 224266 was installed in Fgst.Nr.404572 for a Sfl. 2cm Flak (Sd.Kfz.10/5) completed by M.W.C. about May 1944.

On 1 August 1942, Auto-Union AG, Werk Horch reported having received a contract for 3500 Maybach HL 42 TRKM engines for D 7 with air-brake compressors. Starting with the first 10 in September 1942, Auto-Union completed 460 HL 42 engines (all HL 42 TRKM) in 1942, 8230 in 1943 (of which 2175 were HL 42 TRKM), 10051 in 1944 (of which 1115 were HL 42 TRKM), and 1462 in 1945. Auto-Union A.G. used Motor Nr.700001 to 701982 for HL 42 TRKM produced for D 7 chassis and as of 1 September 1943 switched to a new serial numbering system starting with Motor Nr.2 hul 2241 for HL 42 TRKM.

5.2.2 SRG 102 128 Transmission

On 7 July 1937, Maybach, Friedrichshafen, reported on the status of the semi-automatic transmissions that it had designed. Zahnradfabrik (Z.F.), had received contracts for 1380 Serienausführung (production model) SRG 102 128 (to be used with Motor NL 38) with delivery to begin at the rate of 25 per month in February 1938. Maybach was to complete drawings by 10 September 1938 for a SRG 1021 28 H (Motor NL 38) with hollow shaft for the Lilliput design for which Büssing-NAG, Berlin-Oberschöneweide, had received contracts to produce 300. The hollow shaft in these transmissions was for providing power to auxiliary equipment like spreaders and compressors mounted on le.Entgiftungskw. (Sd.Kfz.10/2) (light decontamination vehicles) and le.Sprühkw. (Sd.Kfz.10/3) (light spray vehicles). According to the replacement parts list, the SRG 102 128 H became the standard transmission, so that a second type did not need to be produced for special applications.

Six assembly plants were licensed by Maybach to produce SRG 102 128 transmissions and 1848 were completed by Z.F., 1403 by Büssing, 9076 by Adler, 1210 by ZF-Augsburg, 2020 by Österreichische Automobil Fabrik A.G., Wien, and 1410 by NAG for a total of 16,967 by 31 March 1943.

Adlerwerke, Frankfurt, reported producing D 7 Getriebe (gearbox) at the rate of 1137 in 1939, 1699 in 1940, 2285 in 1941, 2435 in 1942, and 2399 in 1943, and the last 80 in January 1944 for a total of 10,035.

Tests were carried out at St. Johann involving the fitting of a Schneepflug (snow plough). The Notek light was placed on a raised pedestal and other winter equipment such as the radiator and engine shroud were added. (MA)

D 7 Fahrgestell Production Based on Sonderausschuss Reports

Wa J Rü

Month	Demag	Adler	Büssing	M.W.C.	M.N.H.	Saurer	Total	WaA Accepted
Apr-Jun42	53	235	5	190	10	245	**738**	738
Jul42	24	51	0	70	10	70	**225**	225
Aug42	0	50	5	80	10	85	**230**	230
Sep42	35	52	6	80	5	100	**278**	278
Oct42	14	41	6	70	13	80	**224**	224
Nov42	9	67	10	80	8	80	**254**	254
Dec42	0	52	18	80	0	110	**260**	260
Jan43		55	0	90		100	**245**	240
Feb43		55		110		100	**265**	265
Mar43		55		110		100	**265**	265
Apr43		55		110		100	**265**	265
May43		40		110		100	**250**	250
Jun43		40		110		105	**255**	255
Jul43		40		100		100	**240**	240
Aug43		25		95		100	**220**	220
Sep43		35		120		100	**255**	255
Oct43		0		100		100	**200**	200
Nov43				85		63	**148**	148
Dec43				115		6	**121**	121
Jan44				116		0	**116**	116
Feb44				70			**70**	70
Mar44				150			**150**	150
Apr44				70			**70**	70
May44				130			**130**	130
Jun44				115			**115**	115
Jul44				55			**55**	55
Aug44				25			**25**	25
Sep44				25			**25**	25
Oct44				27			**27**	27
Nov44				108			**108**	108
Dec44				0			**0**	0
Jan45								0
Feb45								80*
Mar45								0
Total	135	948	50	2796	56	1844	3229	3309

*80 issued directly to the troops.

Above: A le.Zgkw.1t (Sd.Kfz.10) with a D 7 chassis completed by Saurerwerke in 1940 with normal 6.00-20 Luftbereifung (tyres with inner tubes) instead of 6.00-20 Lukareifen (tubeless tyres), reinforced A-Rad AS 5114 (outer roadwheel) and I-Rad und Leitrad 021 B 26856U9 (inner roadwheel and idler wheel), and a compressed air tank for the brakes mounted on the rear. (MZ)

Below: A verstärkter (reinforced) le.Zgkw.1t (Sd.Kfz.10) Ausf.B with a reinforced Wanne for towing heavier loads, such as the 10.5cm le.F.H. (light howitzer), 5cm Pak 38 (anti-tank gun) or 15cm s.I.G.33 (heavy infantry gun). Some of the reinforcement, absent on earlier versions, can be seen angling up to the towing bracket. (TA)

Above: A verstärkter le.Zgkw.1t (Sd.Kfz.10) Ausf.B towing a 5cm Pak 38 while training at Cottbus. (PW)
Below: A verstärkter le.Zgkw.1t (Sd.Kfz.10) Ausf.B at the Büssing-NAG design centre in Berlin. (NARA)

6. Modifications during Production

The drawing list on page 22-1-10 represents the initial configuration of the D 7. By March 1941, about 45% of the original components had been altered or superseded as revealed from the following list extracted from the Ersatzteilliste (Replacement Parts List) D672/4 dated 3 March 1941:

AS 5507	**Wanne** (hull)	
HL 42 TRKM	**Maybach Motor** (Maybach engine)	
SRG 102 128 H	**Schaltgetriebe** (transmission)	
AS 5733	**Lenkgetriebe** (steering unit)	
021 E 26853	**Lenkgetriebe** (steering unit)	
021 F 26854	**Kettenantrieb** (track drive)	
021 B 26861	**Blattfeder** (leaf spring)	
021 B 26856	**Laufradschwinge** (swing arms)	
021 C 26856	**Äußeres Laufrad** (outer roadwheel)	
AS 5114	**Äußeres Laufrad** (outer roadwheel)	
021 C 26856	**Inneres Laufrad** (inner roadwheel)	
021 C 26856U9	**Inneres Laufrad** (inner roadwheel)	
021 B 26858	**Leitradschwinge** (idler arm)	
AS 5205/6	**Kotflügel** (fender)	
021 B 26867	**Lampenhalter** (light holder)	
AS 5299	**Lampenhalter** (light holder)	
AS 5513	**Schutzblech für Auspuff** (heat guard)	
021 B 26867U64	**Verkleidung mit Luftkanal** (cover with ventilation channel)	
021 B 26869-141	**Brennstoffbehälter** 110 l (fuel tank)	
021 B 26873	**Anhängerkupplung** (tow pintle)	
021 B 33334	**Kettenglied Zgw.51/240/160** (track link)	
AS 5304	**Sonderaufbau** (special upper body for Sfl. 2cm Flak)	

The following are the significant changes noted in D672/4 dated 5 September 1939, identified by when they were reported as implemented by each assembly plant.

The Wanne 247509 (sheet metal hull) used by Büssing up to Fgst.Nr.300641 was changed to Wanne 021 B 26860 at Fgst.Nr.300642. Wanne 021 B 26860 had been used by all the rest of the assembly firms starting with their first D 7. The radiator cover labelled as part 021 B 26866U4 was introduced by Büssing-NAG starting with Fgst.Nr.300642 at the same time that they changed to a standard Wanne. The Wannenbug 021 B 26860U47 (front end of the hull) used by M.W.C. starting with Fgst.Nr.400401 was changed to 021 B 26860U82 starting with Fgst.Nr.401421.

The protective coverings in front of the front axles and the shock absorbers (part 021 D 26860U15) were used by M.W.C. up to Fgst.Nr.400400 and changed to part 021 D 26860U55 starting with Fgst.Nr.400401. The front springs (part 021 B 26861) were introduced at Adler with Fgst.Nr.201581 (October 1940) and at Büssing with Fgst. Nr.300185.

The strengthened A-Rad AS 5114 (outer roadwheel), I-Rad und Leitrad 021 B 26856U9 (inner roadwheel and idler wheel) were introduced at Demag with Fgst.Nr.00839, Adler with Fgst.Nr.201581 (October 1940), Büssing with Fgst.Nr.300642, M.W.C. with Fgst.Nr. 400401, M.I.A.G. with Fgst.Nr.500011, M.N.H. with Fgst.Nr.600244, and Saurer with Fgst.Nr.700001.

Part 021 B 26866U4 cover for ventilation channel (on the left side of the engine compartment) was changed at Demag starting with Fgst.Nr.100839, Adler with Fgst.Nr.201255 (May 1940), Büssing with Fgst.Nr.300642, M.W.C. with Fgst.Nr.400201, M.I.A.G. with Fgst.Nr.500011, M.N.H. with Fgst.Nr.600119, and Saurer with Fgst.Nr.700001.

A 110-litre Kraftstoffbehälter (fuel tank) replaced the two 58-litre and 31-litre fuel tanks at Demag starting with Fgst.Nr.100401, Adler with Fgst.Nr.200241 (April 1939), Büssing with Fgst.Nr.300012, M.W.C. with Fgst. Nr.400201, M.I.A.G. with Fgst.Nr.500011, M.N.H. with Fgst.Nr.600119, and Saurer with Fgst.Nr.700001.

The 135035/8 floor plates between the Sitzkästen (seat bins) and 235029/32 floor hatches were changed at Demag after Fgst.Nr.100200 and at Adler starting with Fgst. Nr.201255 (May 1940), M.W.C. with Fgst Nr.400201, M.I.A.G. with Fgst.Nr.500011, M.N.H. with Fgst. Nr.600001, and Saurer with Fgst.Nr.700001.

The following changes, listed in chronological order, were also introduced during the production run of the le.Zgkw.1t (Sd.Kfz.10) Typ D 7.

6.1 Notek Tarnscheinwerfer and Abstandrücklicht (Notek Blackout Headlight and Distance Marker Rear Light)

On 30 June 1939, O.K.H./A.H.A./In 6 announced that a Kraftfahrzeug-Nachtmarschgerät (vehicle blackout equipment for night marches), consisting of a Tarnscheinwerfer (Notek covered headlight), an Abstandrücklicht (distance marker tail-light), a second Schlusslicht (tail-light), and a multiple position switch was now commercially available and accepted as standard equipment.

6.2 Maybach HL 42 TRKM (High-Performance Engine)

Starting with Motor Nr.53101, Maybach switched from NL 38 TRKM to HL 42 TRKM production in late 1939. The HL 42 was virtually the same engine as the NL 38; it had simply been bored out to increase the cylinder diameter to create a larger swept volume of 4.192 litres in order to increase the power output from 90 to 100 horsepower at 2800 rpm. A le.Zgkw.1t (Sd.Kfz.10) D 7 produced by Büssing with Fgst.Nr.300111 had one of the last NL 38 TRKM with Motor Nr.53061. A Gasspürkw. (Sd.Kfz.10/1) produced by M.I.A.G. with Fgst.Nr.600063 had one of the first Maybach HL 42 TRKM engines with Motor Nr.53199.

6.3 Verstärkter (Reinforced) Zgkw.1t (Sd.Kfz.10) Ausf.B

In plans for future production, the Heereswaffenamt reported on 3 May 1940:

Only the verstärkter Ausführung (strengthened model) of the Zgkw.1t (Sd.Kfz.10) will be needed. The previous model is dropped. The The Verstärkter Ausf.B is intended for towing the 10.5cm le.F.H., the 5cm Pak38, and the 15cm s.I.G. As a temporary expedient until the Ausf.B is ready, the previous unstrengthened construction will continue in production. All means are to be employed to get the Ausf.B into production, since an urgent need exists.

And, on 18 May 1940:

1t Zgkw. strengthened version (with pneumatic brakes) - As regards pneumatic brakes, there still is no information. Drawings for installation are scheduled to be available at Demag on 1 June 1940. Delivery of 1t Zgkw. with reinforced rear is scheduled to start with 40 in June 1940, 70 in July, and 125 in August.

The reinforced hull rear was introduced by Büssing-NAG starting with Fgst.Nr.300413 and by M.I.A.G. starting with Fgst.Nr.500143.

6.4 Luftkammerreifen (Lukareifen) (Air Chamber Tubeless Tyres)

On 14 September 1940, A.H.A./AgK/M announced that in future, the le Zgkw.1t (Sd.Kfz.10) D 7 will be delivered with normal 6.00-20 Luftbereifung (tyres with inflatable inner tubes) instead of the puncture-proof 6.00-20 Lukareifen.

6.5 Wanne (Hulls) made from 4mm Thick Steel

On 26 November 1940, an announcement in the A.H.M. (General Army Bulletin) informed units that Zgkw.1t (Sd. Kfz.10) mit 2mm steel hulls were to be exchanged for ones made with 4mm steel. Those with a 2mm steel hull were identified as: Demag Fgst.Nr.100001-100189, 100191, 100259, 100278, 100733-100738; Adlerwerke Fgst.Nr. 200001-200030; and M.W.C. Fgst.Nr.400001-400065, 400067-400113, 400115, 400117-400121, 400125, 400126, and 400128-400200.

6.6 Höchstgeschwindigkeit (Maximum Speed) 30 km/hr

On 5 January 1942, the Luftwaffe In 6 (Technical Directorate) announced:

The previous speeds at which Zugmaschinen have been driven has led to the unacceptable condition in which Gummipolster (rubber track pads) are rapidly wearing out. The maximum allowable speed limit that immediately goes into effect for all Sd.Kfz. with Zgkw.-Fahrgestell including variants, is 30 km/ hr. This speed limit is not applicable for combat troops when the tactical situation requires higher speed.

6.7 Compressed Air Tank for Air Brakes with Hose Coupling

For towing heavier loads, such as a 7.5cm Pak, which was fitted with air brakes, the le.Zgkw.1t (Sd.Kfz.10) with D 7 Fahrgestell was outfitted with a Bremsluftbehälter mit Schlauchkupplung (compressed air tank with hose coupling). The compressed air tank was filled by a Luftpresser Knorr V 6.9/80 (air compressor) driven by a belt from the Maybach HL 42 TRKM engine. For example, le.Zgkw.1t (Sd.Kfz.10) with Fgst.Nr.701602 completed by Saurer-Werke about September 1942 was outfitted for loads that had air brakes. The track guards had welded-on extensions to protect the compressed air tank mounted across the rear.

6.8 Fahrtrichtungsanzeiger (Turn Signals)

As announced by the Luftwaffe In 6 on 23 March 1943, the Fahrtrichtungsanzeiger were no longer to be installed on vehicles for the rest of the war.

6.9 Stahlkappen (Steel Caps on Tracks)

Wa Prüf 6 tested the le.Zgkw.1t D 7 Fgst.Nr.500271 with Zgw.53/240/160 mit Stahlkappen, Zgw.53/240/160,

Zpw.53/240/150 with W 102 Serienpolster (standard rubber pads, and Zgw.53/240/150 tracks with Notlaufpolster W 112g (emergency rubber pads) on hard surfaces.

On 4 June 1943, Wa J Rü (Wu G) informed the Waffenamt that the production of Gleiskette (track links) for Zgkw.1t and 3t would be converted to rubber-free, steel-capped tracks.

As announced in the Heeres-Technisches-Verordnungs-Blatt (Army Technical Directive Circular) by Wa Prüf 6 on 24 February 1944:

Instead of the previous tracks with rubber pads tracks - designated as steel running tracks - will be issued with Stahlkappen in the future. The maximum speed of vehicles with steel capped tracks is to be limited to 30 km/hr on the road. Exceeding this speed causes damage to the tracks and suspension components. Increased danger of skidding exists on smooth, slick roads. Off-road, the steel capped tracks act the same as tracks with rubber pads.

Like the steel-capped tracks for the m.Schtz.Pz.Wg. (Sd. Kfz.251), the Stahllaufketten for the le.Schtz.Pz.Wg. (Sd. Kfz.250) and Zgkw.1t (Sd.Kfz.10) were used for only a short period.

6.10 Hauptscheinwerfer (Headlight)

On 15 October 1943, the Heereswaffenamt Sparkommissar (Austerity Commissioner) announced that the following applied to special-purpose vehicles of the Wehrmacht:

Effective immediately, Zugkraftwagen are to now have two commercial Scheinwerfer (headlights) and a Tarnscheinwerfer (capped blackout headlight). Seitenleuchte (side lights) are to be discontinued.

6.11 Renk-Schaltung (Mechanical Shifting) for the VG 102 128 H Transmission

Instructions for converting a Variorexgetriebe 102 128 H from Maybach semi-automatic vacuum-assisted shifting to mechanical Renk-Schaltung shifting were prepared by Wa Prüf 6 on 1 December 1944. This modification had already occurred much earlier in newly produced D 7 Fahrgestell at the assembly plants, sometime between July and October 1943.

6.12 Pritschen-Aufbau (Flatbed Upper Bodies)

Starting 1943, in an effort to save on steel, it was planned to replace the metal upper bodies for the entire Zugkraftwagen series from 1t to 18t with Pritschen-Aufbau made from wood. By 1944, M.W.C. was the sole supplier of D 7, and in March 1944, it was reported that le.Zgkw.1t were being completed with wooden superstructures, so at least he last 90 D 7's were built in that fashion, although the switch could actually have occurred in 1943.

6.13 Projects

6.13.1 le.Zgkw.1t D 8

In 1939, the D 8 project was initiated for a le.Zgkw.1t with extended trackwork. One extra torsion bar was to be added. The only other change was to be a new model of the Maybach Variorex pre-selector gearbox with 8 rather than 7 speeds. The D 8 project was cancelled.

6.13.2 Verstärktes Laufwerk (Strengthened Running Gear) le.Zgkw.1t

In 1944, Demag was awarded contract SS 4935-0006- 1614/44 by Wa Prüf 6 to produce three Verstärkter le.Zgkw.1t. This contract is not to be confused with the Verstärkter Zgkw.1t (Sd.Kfz.10) Ausf.B (described in 6.3). The three new Verstärkter le.Zgkw.1t were to have 10 roadwheels, strengthened front axle, strengthened idler crank arm) improved track tensioner, and raised ground clearance. Demag met the requested schedule by completing two in September and the third in October 1944. The first two were delivered in September 1944, but the third Versuchs-Maschine remained at the assembly plant.

6.13.3 Pritschenwagen (Flatbed Vehicle) on the D 7p Fahrgestell (Sd.Kfz.250 Chassis) and New Model with Longer Running Gear

On 2 February 1945, in response to the deteriorating situation, the Sonderausschuss decided:

Due to the loss of important areas in the East and the West, delivery of components to the assembly firms is no longer secure. Therefore, the current situation and resulting production capability were discussed with the assembly plants and Wehrmacht.

1t Zgkw.: At Demag, Wetter/Ruhr, there are 150 Pz.-Wannen (D 7p armour hulls for the Sd.Kfz.250) in storage and another 200 in the assembly hall for a total of 350. At M.W.C. Cottbus, there are 200 Pz.-Wannen in storage and another 50 in the assembly hall for a total of 250. There are 324 Panzer-Aufbau (armour superstructures) at the Sd.Kfz.250 assembler, Evens u. Pistor, Helsa bei Kassel, and another 80 available from the Panzer-Nebenzeugamt Olmütz. O.K.H. (WuG6) will determine if this is true and attempt to get these 80 Aufbau sent to Evens u. Pistor.

Considering this available inventory, production of the le.S.P.W. is certain only through the end of March 1945. After this, starting in April 1945, the 1t Zgkw. can be completed only as Pritschenwagen. Demag and M.W.C. were informed that starting in April, the 1t Zgkw. is to be completed in accordance with the new design developed by Demag with a lengthened Laufwerk (longer suspension). As long as the assembly plants still have Panzerwanne, these are to be used at the start of the neue Serie (new series) to make Pritschenfahrzeuge (vehicles with wooden upper bodies).

The following production is planned. Demag is to complete 100 Fahrgestell by 15 February and another 100 by the end of the month. M.W.C. is to complete 104 Fahrgestell by 10 February and another 100 by the end of the month. If transport is available, all 404 should be sent to Evens und Pistor in February 1945.

M.W.C. reported that the Rüstungs-Kommando Frankfurt/Oder had ordered M.W.C. to provide the already completed D 7p Fahrgestell for the withdrawal of the Luftwaffe stationed in Cottbus. This will interfere with delivering these Fahrgestell to Evens und Pistor. WuG 6 Oberst v. Wilke will follow this situation and will report how delivery of these commandeered Fahrgestell can occur.

On 28 February 1945, 354 Pritschen-Aufbau Sd.Kfz.10 on D 7p Fahrgestell were scheduled to be completed under the Notprogramm 1945 (emergency program):

Demag was to complete 126 (26 in March and 100 in April), and M.W.C. was to complete 228 (78 in February that had already been given directly to the troops and 150 in March).

Wa J Rü independently reported that 80 had been given directly to the troops as towing vehicles in February 1945 with plans to complete another 176 in March and 100 in April.

6.13.4 1t Zgkw. mit gepanzertem Motor und gepanzerten Fahrerfront (with Armoured Engine and Driver Compartments)

Under the Entwicklungs-Notprogramm (development emergency program) dated 20 February 1945, the Chef des Heeresstabes Rüst informed Wa Chef Prüf that future development had been divided into three categories. Listed as item 23 in category 1 was development of a 1t Zgkw. mit gepanzertem Motor und gepanzerten Fahrerfront that was planned to be completed in June 1945. Category 1 items were weapons/vehicles being developed that would have a decisive influence on the war, could be finished within the foreseeable future, and had to be accomplished under the highest priority.

This verstärkter le.Zgkw.1t (Sd.Kfz.10) Ausf.B with a reinforced Wanne (hull) towing a 7.5cm le.I.G.18 was issued as a replacement for a le.S.P.W. (Sd.Kfz.250). (JW)

Above: Starting with Kriegsstärkenachweis (Tables of Organisation and Equipment) dated 1 February 1941 and continuing to early 1944, le.Zgkw.1t (Sd.Kfz.10) were assigned to the vehicle repair sections of most Panzer-Kompanien. (HB)

Below: When German forces from the Ruhr Pocket surrendered near Menden, they left behind two le.Zgkw.1t (Sd.Kfz.10) Ausf.B mit Pritschen-Aufbau. These 1944 vehicles also featured small commercial headlights and were not fitted with turn signals or a rear-view mirror. (NARA)

7. Organisation and Issue

Based on the earliest photographs from 1935/36, the Lilliput, later renamed le.Zgkw.1t (Sd.Kfz.10), was intended to be employed for towing the 2cm Flak, 3.7cm Pak, 7.5cm le.I.G., and Sonder-Anhänger (special ammunition trailers). Its role was expanded in 1939 to being used as a substitute for the planned leichter gepanzerter Mannschafts-Transport-Kraftwagen (light, armoured Personnel Transport Vehicle) (Sd.Kfz.250) and in 1940 for towing the heavier 5cm Pak 38, 10.5cm le.F.H.18, and 15cm s.I.G.33, for which the reinforced le.Zgkw.1t (Sd.Kfz.10) Ausf.B was created. Starting in late 1940, the le.Zgkw.1t (Sd.Kfz.10) were also issued to Kfz.Instandsetzung (vehicle repair) sections. A unique role was nine le.Zgkw.1t (Sd.Kfz.10) as Gefechtskraftwagen. (combat vehicles) armed with 8.8cm Raketen-Panzerbüchse 54 in Type 'c' armoured reconnaissance battalions organised under Kriegsstärkenachweis (K.St.N.1112c) (Table of Organisation & Equipment), dated 1 November 1943. Due to the widespread usage of the le.Zgkw.1t (Sd.Kfz.10), the organisations are grouped under their assigned role.

7.1 Substitute for le.gp.M.T.Kw. (Sd.Kfz.250)

As revealed in the first set of K.St.N. dated 19 October 1939 for Schützen-Regiment 1 (Motorised Rifle Regiment 1), the unarmoured le.Zgkw.1t (Sd.Kfz.10) was authorised as a substitute for the (Sd.Kfz.250).

On 18 October 1939, O.K.H./A.H.A./In 6 reported that Schtz.Rgt.1 in 1.Panzer-Division was to be completely outfitted with light and medium personnel transport vehicles (Sd.Kfz.10 and Sd.Kfz.251 - armoured and unarmoured) (light and medium personnel carriers both armoured and unarmoured). These K.St.N. specified le.gp.M.T.Kw.(Sd.Kfz.250) but there were footnotes that Sd.Kfz.10 were authorised substitutes. A total of 90 Sd.Kfz.10 were issued to fill the following elements:

Unit	K.St.N.	Sd.Kfz.10
Stb.Schtz.Brig	-	1
Rgts.Stb.Schtz.Rgt.1	1104gp	1
Nachr.Zug Schtz.Rgt.1	1197gp	8
Stb.I./Schtz.Rgt.1	1108gp	8
Schtz.Kp.I.Btl.	1114gp	2
Schtz.Kp.I.Btl.	1114gp	2
M.G.Kp.I.Btl.	1116gp	8
Fhr.Gr.s.Kp.I.Btl.	1121gp	1
Pak-Zug s.Kp.I.Btl.	1122gp	5
Gesch.Zug s.Kp.I.Btl.	1123gp	2
Pi.Zug s.Kp.I.Btl.	1124gp	1
II./Schtz.Rgt.1	same as I.Btl.	29
Stb.III./Schtz.Rgt.1	1108gp	8
3 Schtz.Kp.	1114gp	6
M.G.Kp.III.Btl.	1116gp	8

A le.Zgkw.1t (Sd.Kfz.10) showing its capability for climbing while towing a 3.7cm Pak. (PW)

The 17 Sd.Kfz.10 with racks for kl.Fernspr.Tr.c mot (Motorised Telephone Section), 8 with racks for Torn Fu.Tr.b mot 1 (radios), 8 with racks for Pz.Fu.Tr.d mot (radios), and 10 with holders for Pak Munition had been outfitted already with the racks and holders at Heeres-Zeugamt Spandau (Army Equipment Centre Spandau). A total of 61 Sd.Kfz.10 were already available with Schtz.Rgt.1, and 29 remained to be sent fromSpandau, of which 26 had Fernspr. und Fu Gerät (telephone and radio equipment). In addition, eight rifle racks were already installed in the Sd.Kfz.10. The unit was reminded to obey the then maximum speed limit of 45 km/hr for the Sd.Kfz.10.

The footnote that Sd.Kfz.10 were authorised substitutes for Sd.Kfz.250 was still applicable in this same K.St.N. series updated on 1 February 1941. The le.Zgkw.1t (Sd.Kfz.10) were issued as substitutes until mass production of the le.S.P.W. (Sd.Kfz.250) started in June 1941.

7.2 Towing 3.7cm Pak and 5cm Pak 38

The 3.7cm Pak were to be towed by m.gl.Pkw. mit Zugvorrichtung (Kfz.12) (medium off-road cars with towing equipment) or Protze (Kfz.69) (motorised limber) in accordance with Pz.Abw.Kp. K.St.N.184 v.1Oct37, Pz.Abw.Kp.a (mot Z) K.St.N.1141 v.1Oct37, Pz.Jg.Zug in s.Kp. K.St.N.1122 v.1Oct37 and 1Feb41, and Pz.Jg.Kp. K.St.N.184c v.31Jan41.

On 19 November 1940, O.K.H./A.H.A./In6 announced in the A.H.M. the number of 1t Zgkw. (Sd.Kfz.10) for towing 3.7cm and 5cm Pak authorised in a Panzer-Division and Infanterie-Division (mot) as follows:

Panzer-Division

	3.7cm Pak	5cm Pak 38
Panzerjägerabteilung	36	45
Pak-Zug der Aufkl.Abt.	3	5
Pak-Züge der Schützen-Btl.	12	20
Pak-Zug des Kradsch.Btl.	3	5
Total	54	75

Infanterie-Division (mot) (Motorised Infantry Division)

	3.7cm Pak	5cm Pak 38
Panzerjägerabteilung	36	45
2 Pz.Jg.Kp. der Sch.Rgt.	24	32
Pak-Zug des Kradsch.Btl.	3	5
Pak-Zug der Aufkl.Abt.	3	5
Total	66	87

The le.Zgkw.1t (Sd.Kfz.10) was authorised by K.St.N./K.A.N. Kriegsausrüstungsnachweisung (Tables of Distribution and Allowances) to be assigned to Panzer-Jäger units to tow the anti-tank guns and ammunition trailers, such as:

3 in **Inf.Pz.Jg.Zug** (3 3.7 Pak), K.St.N.188e, 1Dec41
3 in **Pz.Jg.Kp.**(4.7cm)(mot S) K.St.N.1148, 1Nov41
5 in **gem.Pz.Jg.Kp.** (3 Pak 38) K.St.N.1142, 1Nov41
5 in **Stbs.Kp.Schtz.Rgts.** K.St.N.1153, 1Nov41
5 in **Pz.Jg.Zug in s.Kp.** (3 Pak 38) K.St.N.1122, 1Dec41
9 in **Gebirgsjäger-Kp.**(mot Z) K.St.N.187, 1Nov41
9 in **Inf.Pz.Jg.Kp.a** (mot Z), K.St.N.184a, 1Nov41
12 in **Inf.Pz.Jg.Kp.c** (mot Z), K.St.N.184c, 1Nov41
15 in **Pz.Jg.Kp.**(9 Pak 38)(mot Z), K.St.N.1144, 1Nov41
18 in **s.Pz.Jg.Kp.**(9 7.5 or 7.6)(mot Z), K.St.N.1140, 1Jun42

Early in 1943, the following K.St.N. were amended by an announcement in the A.H.M.:

K.St.N.1140 v.1Jun42
6 Maultier (Sd.Kfz.3) in place of 9 le.Zgkw.(1t) (Sd.Kfz.10)
K.St.N.1142 v.1Nov41
2 or 4 Maultier (Sd.Kfz.3) in place of 2 or 4 le.Zgkw.(1t) (Sd.Kfz.10)
K.St.N.1144 v.1Nov41
6 Maultier (Sd.Kfz.3) in place of 6 le.Zgkw.(1t) (Sd.Kfz.10)
K.St.N.1145 v.22Jan42
2 Maultier (Sd.Kfz.3) in place of 3 le.Zgkw.(1t) (Sd.Kfz.10)
K.St.N.1149a v.1Feb42
2 Maultier (Sd.Kfz.3) in place of 1 le.Zgkw.(1t) (Sd.Kfz.10)

7.3 Towing 7.5cm le.I.G. and 15cm s.I.G

The 7.5cm le.I.G. (infantry gun) was normally towed by a m.gl.Pkw. mit Zugvorrichtung (Kfz.12) (medium off-road cars with towing equipment) or a Protze (Kfz.69) (motorised limber) in accordance with le.I.G.Kp. K.St.N.173 v.1Oct37, le.I.G.Zug in s.Kp. (K.St.N.1123 v.1Oct37 and 1Feb41). However, the heavier s.I.G.33 were usually towed by le.Zgkw.1t (Sd.Kfz.10). The le.Zgkw.1t (Sd.Kfz.10) were authorised by K.St.N./K.A.N. to be assigned to Infanterie-Geschütz units to tow the infantry guns and ammunition trailers, such as:

12 in **s.I.G.Kp.** (mot S) K.St.N.179, 30Mar40
14 in **s.I.G.Kp.** (mot Z) K.St.N.120, 1Feb41
4 in **I.G.Kp.** (mot Z) f.2 s.I.G. K.St.N.176,1Nov41
4 in **Gesch.Zug** (2 le.I.G.)(mot Z) K.St.N.1123, 1Nov41
14 in **s.I.G.Kp.** (4 s.I.G.)(mot Z) K.St.N.1120, 1Nov41
10 in **I.G.Kp.**(mot Z)Gr.D.K.St.N.174, 1Dec42
18 in **s.I.G.Kp.**(6 s.I.G.)(mot Z) K.St.N.178, 1May42
13 in **Gesch.Kp.**(6 le.I.G., 2 s.I.G.)(mot) K.St.N.1120b, 1Nov43

7.4 Towing 2cm Flak

The 2cm Flak were normally towed by a Flakmannsch.Kw. (Kfz.81) (flak crew wheeled-vehicle) as specified in K.St.N.191 dated 1Oct37 for the M.G.Kp.(s)(mot Z), later renamed leichte Flakkraftwagen (Sd.Kfz.81) in K.St.N.1713 dated 1Jul42 for the Heeres-Flakbatterie 2cm (12 Geschütze) (mot Z).

7.5 Kraftfahrzeug-Instandsetzung

Starting on 1 February 1941, two le.Zgkw.1t (Sd.Kfz.10) were assigned to the vehicle repair section of the le.Pz.Kp. K.St.N.1171Sd, m.Pz.Kp. K.St.N.1175Sd and Pz.Kp. (Flamm) K.St.N.1177. This practice continued through 1 November 1943 with 28 different Pz.Kp. (including Panthers, Tigers, and Sturmgeschütze) being authorised to have two in the vehicle repair section. In 1943, the practice was to authorise one le.Zgkw.1t (Sd.Kfz.10) to the Kfz.Inst. Gr. (vehicle repair Ssection) in more than 29 different units, mainly Stbs.Kp.Pz.Abt. and Pz.Jg.Kp. with self-propelled guns. Under the freie Gliederung (open structure) concept, starting in March 1944 and continuing through 1945, the le.Zgkw.1t (Sd.Kfz.10) were taken away from the individual Pz. and Pz.Jg.Kp. and consolidated into a Versorgungs-Kompanie (supply company) for the entire Abteilung. For example, nine were authorised for the Versorg.Kp. (f.G.) Pz.Abt. Panther K.St.N.1151a (f.G.) 1Apr44 and seven for the Versorg.Kp.s.Pz.Abt. Tiger (f.G.) K.St.N.1151b (f.G.) 1Jun44.

Operation Barbarossa. Troops of Das Reich equipped with an Adler assembled le.Zgkw.1t (Sd.Kfz.10), entering a Russian village on 25 August 1941. (PW)

Leichter Zugkraftwagen 1t (Sd.Kfz.10) Ausf.A completed in 1938

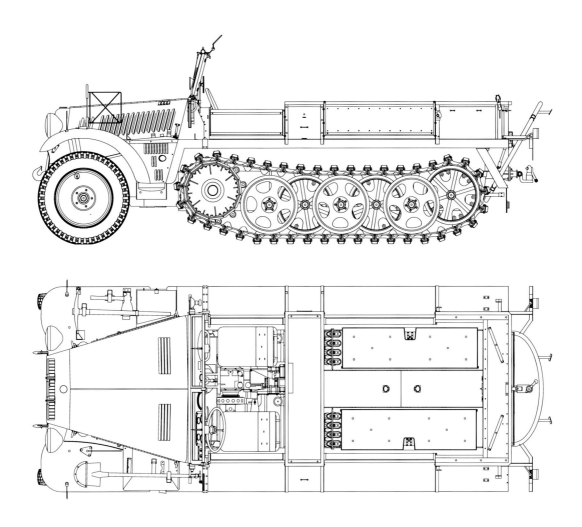

© Copyright. Hilary L. Doyle 2009

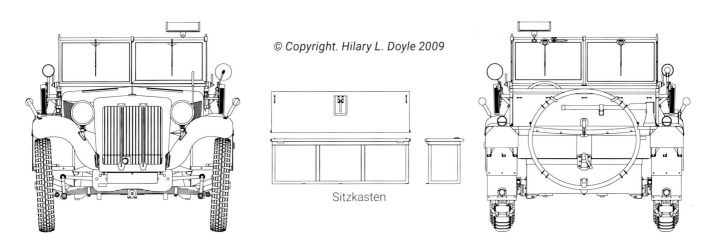

Sitzkasten

Features present on this le.Zgkw.1t (Sd.Kfz.10) Ausf.A include: headlights mounted higher and farther apart, complex ventilation slits in the sides of the bonnet, two fuel tanks, the pre-selector on top of the transmission, twin licence plates, and two tail-lights.

Leichter Zugkraftwagen 1t (Sd.Kfz.10) Ausf.A completed in 1940

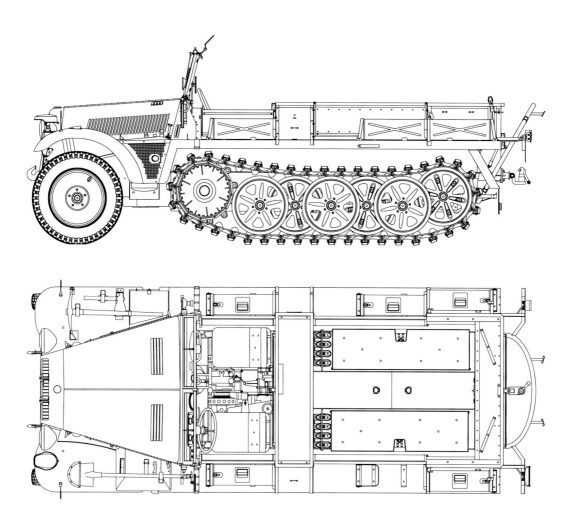

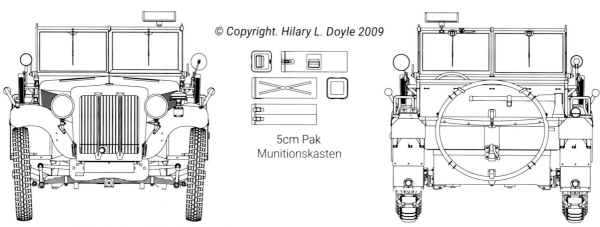

© Copyright. Hilary L. Doyle 2009

5cm Pak
Munitionskasten

Features present on this le.Zgkw.1t (Sd.Kfz.10) Ausf.A completed in 1940 include: convex slits in the sides on the engine bonnet, strengthened A-Rad AS 5114 (outer roadwheel) and I-Rad und Leitrad 021B26856U9 (inner roadwheel and idler wheel), Notek blackout light and convoy tail-light, and a normal tail-light on the right rear. This le.Zgkw.1t is configured to tow a 5cm Pak 38 being equipped with five 5cm Pak Munitionskasten (ammunition containers), each containing four rounds, attached to the track guards.

Leichter Zugkraftwagen 1t (Sd.Kfz.10) Ausf.B completed in 1942

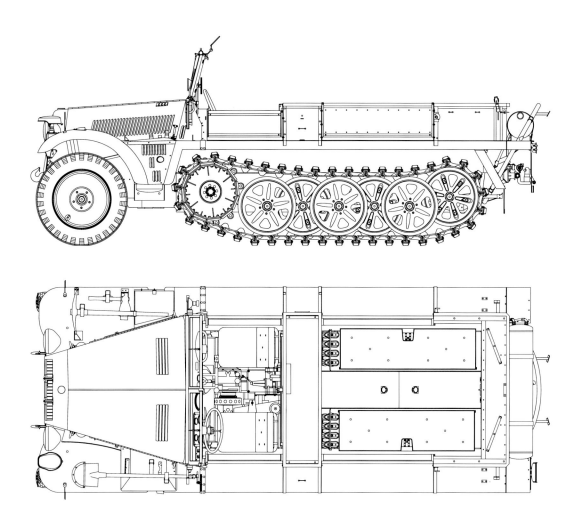

© Copyright. Hilary L. Doyle 2009

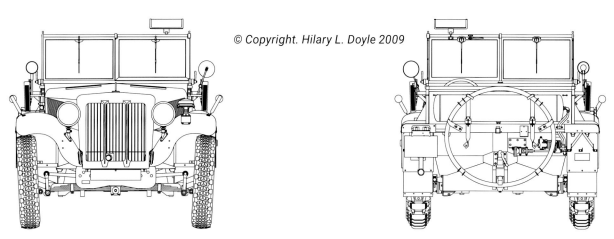

Features present on this le.Zgkw.1t (Sd.Kfz.10) Ausf.B completed in 1942 include: a reinforced hull rear, a compressed air tank with fittings for towing heavier guns with air brakes, extended track guards, a modified mount for the K-Rolle at rear (carrier for roll of barbed wire), the saw holder relocated to the front of the baggage bin behind the driver, and standard 6.00-20 tyres with inner tubes.

Leichter Zugkraftwagen 1t (Sd.Kfz.10) Ausf.B completed in 1942

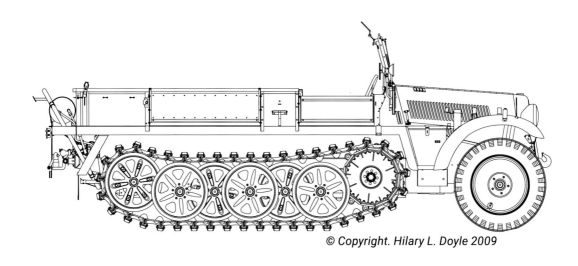

© Copyright. Hilary L. Doyle 2009

Leichter Zugkraftwagen 1t (Sd.Kfz.10) Ausf.B completed in 1942 with Klappverdeck (convertible top) erected and side panels installed

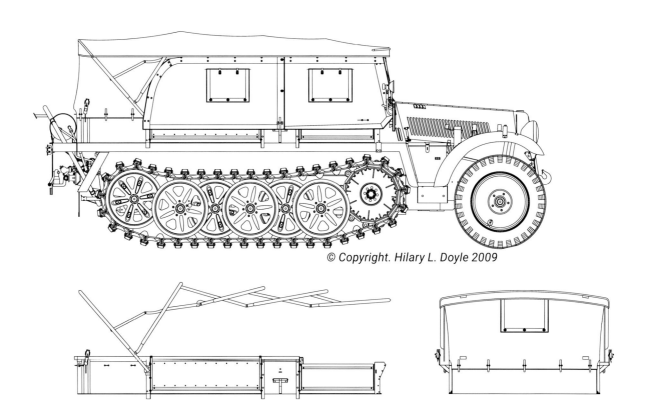

© Copyright. Hilary L. Doyle 2009

Gasspürerkraftwagen (Sd.Kfz.10/1) Ausf.B completed in 1942

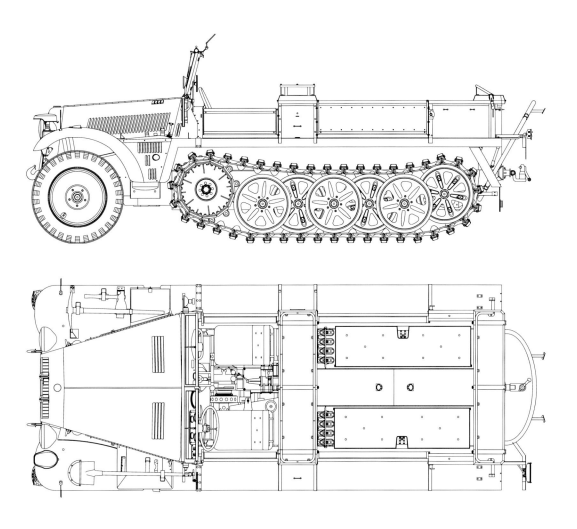

© Copyright. Hilary L. Doyle 2009

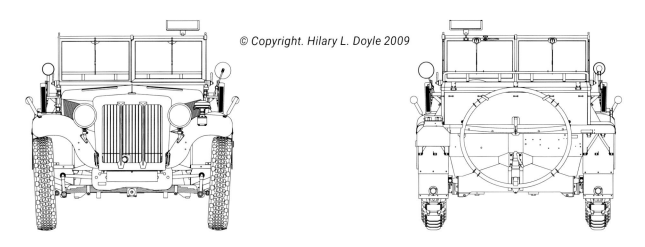

Features present on this poison gas detection vehicle include: a cover over the forward bin and a second stowage bin with a cover fitted at the rear - both covers with hand rails, strengthened roadwheels, standard 6.00-20 tyres with inner tubes, and a reinforced hull rear.

Wanne for a Leichter Zugkraftwagen 1t (Sd.Kfz.10) Ausf.A completed in 1938

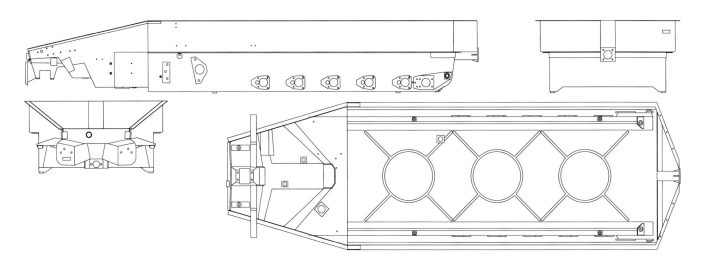

Verstärkte Wanne for a Leichter Zugkraftwagen 1t (Sd.Kfz.10) Ausf.B completed in 1942

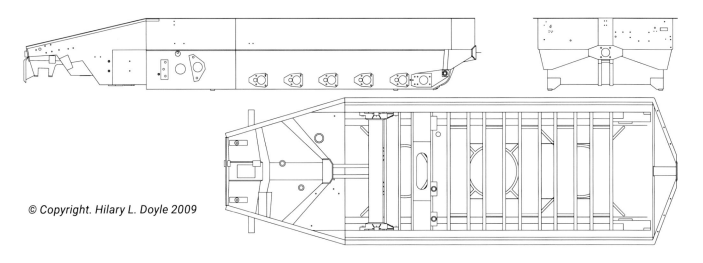

© Copyright. Hilary L. Doyle 2009

Verstärkte Wanne for a Selbstfahrlafette (Sd.Kfz.10/4) completed in 1943

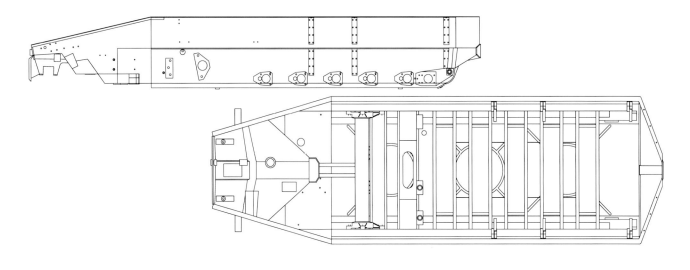

Leichter Entgiftungskraftwagen (Sd.Kfz.10/2) Ausf.A. D 7s completed in 1939

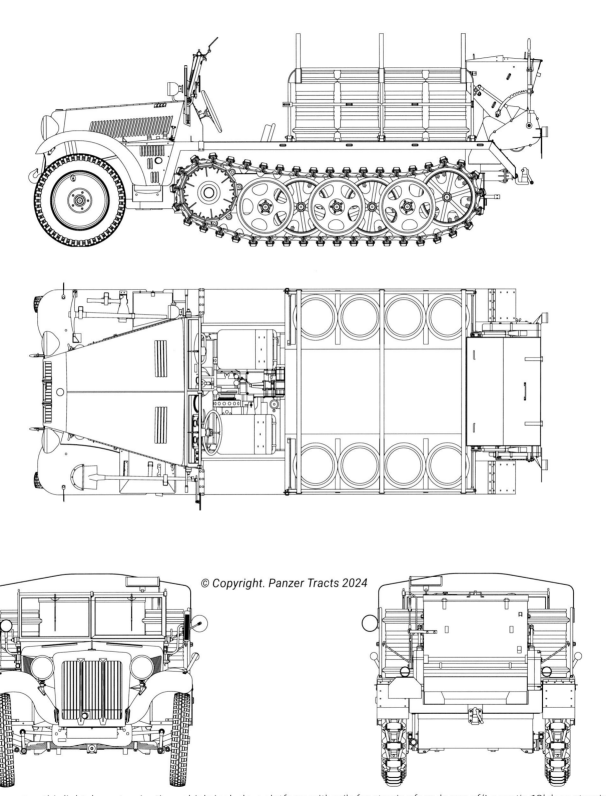

© Copyright. Panzer Tracts 2024

Features present on this light decontamination vehicle include: a platform with rails for stowing four drums of 'Losantin 12' decontaminant on each side and providing a workspace for the crew to load the Streuvorrichtung (spreader) on the rear. This was driven by a transfer shaft from the left of the gearbox. The turn signals along with the mirror were mounted higher and farther apart to clear the load area. A larger searchlight was provided.

2cm Flak 30

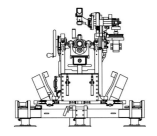
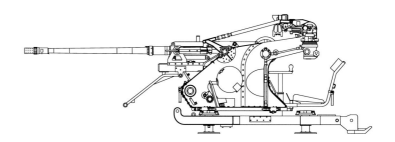

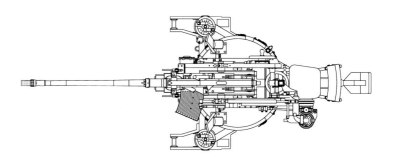

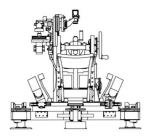
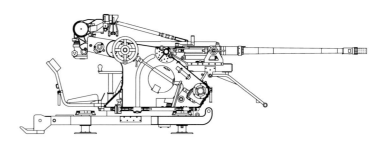

This 2cm Flak 30 was completed in 1939 with a Flakvisier 35 sight and mechanical computer linked to the traverse and elevation mechanisms.

Selbstfahrlafette (Sd.Kfz.10/4) für 2cm Flak 30 completed in 1939

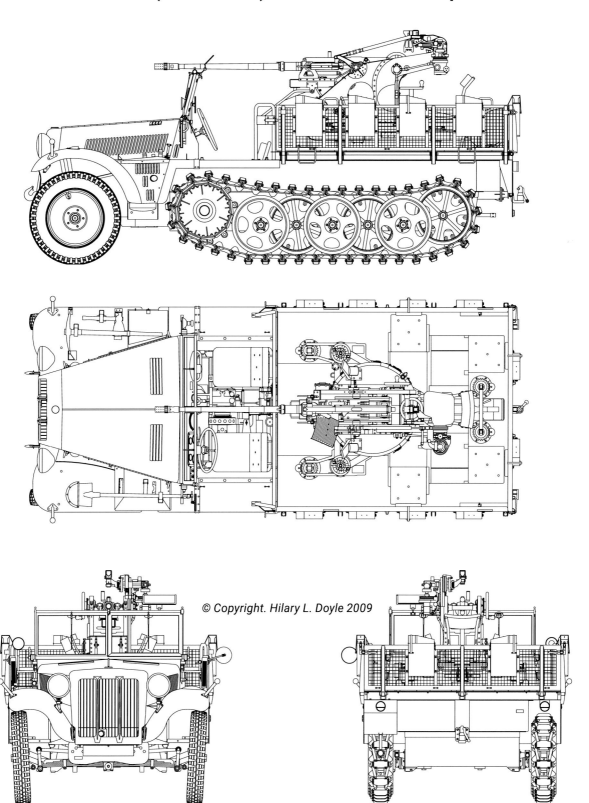

© Copyright. Hilary L. Doyle 2009

Features present on this Sfl.(Sd.Kfz.10/4) für 2cm Flak 30 completed between July and September 1939 include: a 2.27-metre-long by 1.9-metre-wide platform for the 2cm Flak 30, gun crew seats provided by flipping open hatches in the platform, a modified and relocated pre-selector for the transmission, the mirror and turn signals mounted farther out, special 6.00-20 Lukareifen (tyres with air chambers), and an unreinforced Wanne (hull).

Selbstfahrlafette (Sd.Kfz.10/4) für 2cm Flak 30 (mit Auffahrschienen) completed in 1940

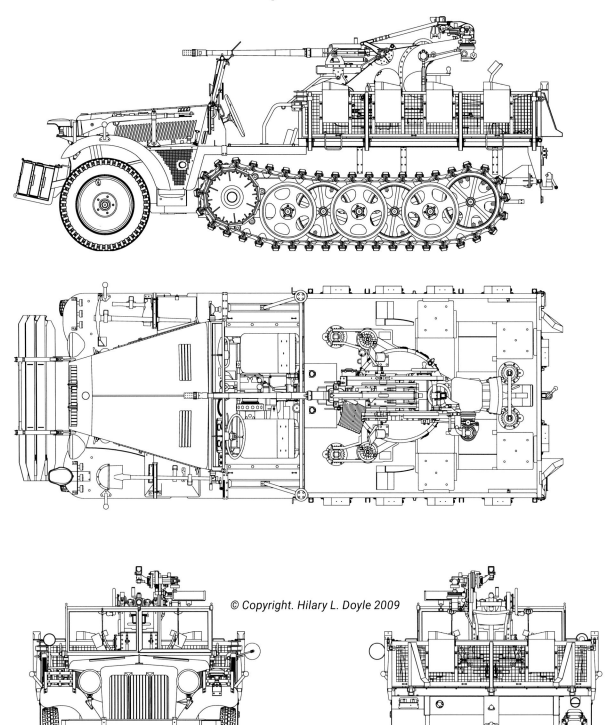

© Copyright. Hilary L. Doyle 2009

Features present on this Sfl.(Sd.Kfz.10/4) für 2cm Flak 30 completed in 1940 include: Auffahrschienen (loading ramps) with Seilrollen (pulleys) and accessories for dismounting the 2cm Flak 30, reinforcing strips on the hull sides, a single fuel tank, handles added to the sides of the dashboard, rifle racks mounted above the front fenders, and a Notek blackout light and convoy tail-light.

Selbstfahrlafette (Sd.Kfz.10/4) für 2cm Flak 30 (mit Auffahrschienen) completed in 1940

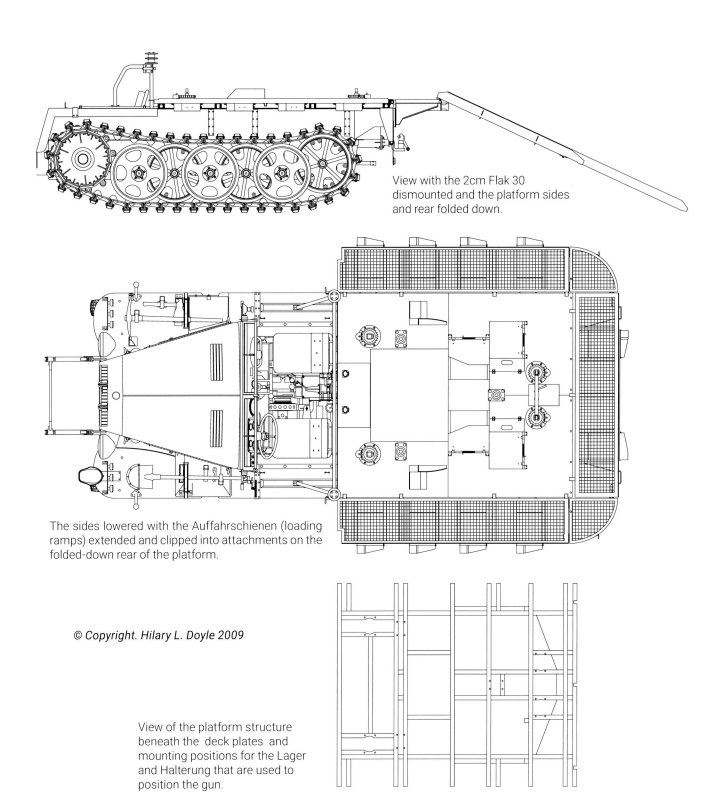

View with the 2cm Flak 30 dismounted and the platform sides and rear folded down.

The sides lowered with the Auffahrschienen (loading ramps) extended and clipped into attachments on the folded-down rear of the platform.

View of the platform structure beneath the deck plates and mounting positions for the Lager and Halterung that are used to position the gun.

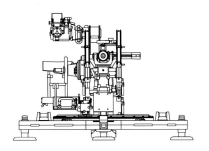

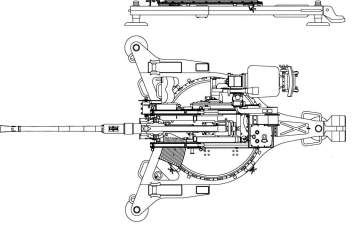

2cm Flak 38 completed in 1942 with a Flakvisier 38a and an electro/mechanical computer linked to the traverse and elevation mechanisms

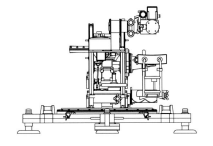

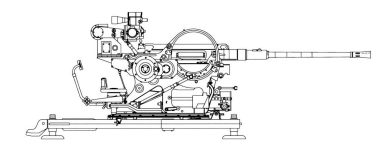

2cm Flak 38 completed in 1943/44 with a Schwebekreisvisier 38 (pendulum ring sight) and simplified construction

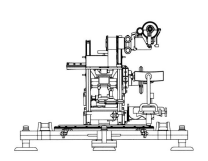

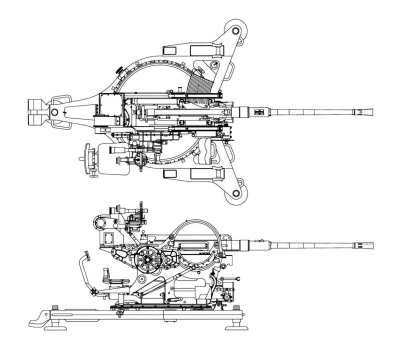

Selbstfahrlafette (Sd.Kfz.10/5) für 2cm Flak 38 mit Behelfspanzerung completed in 1942

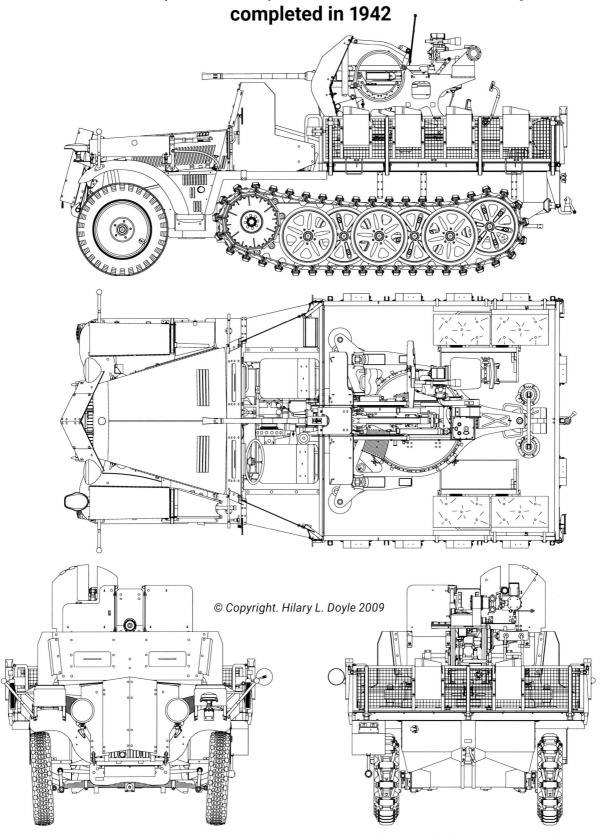

© Copyright. Hilary L. Doyle 2009

Features present on this Sfl. (Sd.Kfz.10/5) für 2cm Flak 38 completed in 1942 include: 8mm thick Behelfspanzerung (expedient armour) backfitted in 1943, a 2.23 metre wide platform for the 2cm Flak 38, covers over the rifle racks, a heat a heat guard above the exhaust muffler, turn signals and rear view mirror mounted farther out, reinforced hull rear, and standard 6.00-20 tyres with inner tubes.

Selbstfahrlafette (Sd.Kfz.10/5) für 2cm Flak 38 completed in 1944

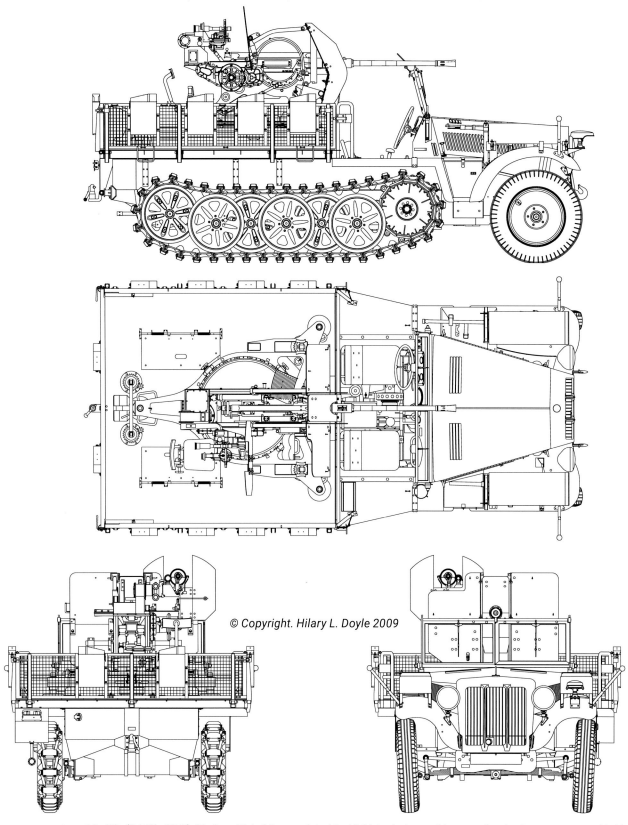

© Copyright. Hilary L. Doyle 2009

Features present on this Sfl. (Sd.Kfz.10/5) für 2cm Flak 38 completed in 1944 include: a wider opening in the upper gun shield for the Schwebekreisvisier 38 (pendulum ring sight), Renk manual shifting for the transmission, turn signals and rear view mirror no longer mounted, and standard 6.00-20 tyres with inner tubes.

9. leichter Nachrichtungskraftwagen (Sd.Kfz.10)

A small series of leichter Nachrichtenkraftwagen (Sd. Kfz.10) were produced with an Aufbau (upper body) that had been specially developed for the needs of Nachrichten (Signals) units using the D 6 chassis (see page 22-1-11). The Aufbau sides were higher than the leichter Zugkraftwagen 1t. Hinged doors were fitted for the driver, co-driver, and at the centre rear for the crew. Büssing-NAG supplied the D 7 chassis.

A leichter Nachrichtenkraftwagen (Sd.Kfz.10) laying schweres Feldkabel (heavy field cables) during a 1941 exercise in Pörtschach, Austria with the Gebirgs-Nachrichten-Abteilung 70. (PW)

Reels of schweres Feldkabel are delivered to the leichter Nachrichtenkraftwagen (Sd. Kfz.10) by a kleines Kettenkrad für schweres Feldkabel (Sd. Kfz.2/2). (PW)

10. Gasspürerkraftwagen (Sd.Kfz.10/1) leichter Entgiftungskraftwagen (Sd.Kfz.10/2) leichter Sprühkraftwagen (Sd.Kfz.10/3)

Despite Germany having ratified the Protocol of 1925 prohibiting the use of poison gas, O.K.H. was aware that other states had reservations about signing this Protocol, so there was a possibility that poison gas might be used in the event of war. The training of German troops in anti-gas defence was therefore considered essential. If gas was used by an enemy, Germany reserved the right to take corresponding retaliatory measures. Plans were therefore laid to create special chemical units (Nebeltruppen) to deal with this threat.

Preliminary plans for unit organisation dated 31 October 1936 reveal that designs had been initiated for three types of vehicles desired by the Nebeltruppen, as follows: The Nebel-Abteilung (mot) was to be organised with three Nb.Batterien and a Nb.Gerät-Kol. (Geländevergiftung). Each Nebel-Batterie had a 1.Zug (Nb. Werferzug) with six Nb.Werfergruppen and a 2. Zug (Geländeentgiftungszug) with four Entgiftungsgruppen. The Nb.Werfergruppe on a m.gl.Lkw. (medium cross-country truck) or kl.gl.Zkw. manned a smooth-bore 10.5cm Nebelwerfer firing smoke or gas munitions at a rate of 12-15 rounds per minute at a maximum range of 3200 metres. The decontamination section was issued either a medium decontamination vehicle or a small cross-country truck with 750 kg of decontamination chemicals, which could spread a 1.7-metre wide strip 1.5 kilometres long. The Nb.Gerät-Kolonne with three platoons each with one kl.gl.Zkw. and two m.Sprüh.Kw. or kl.gl.Zkw. mit Sprühkessel could contaminate a 12-metre wide strip 8 kilometres long.

In May 1938, when O.K.H. was considering the creation of three top-secret chemical battalions that could be activated in the event of war, there were reservations that:

The danger that these units are 'unusable' because they would 'never or only exceptionally be used' was refuted by recent reports that the Czechs want to use Kampfstoff (poison gas) on the first day of war. If these units are not needed for dispersing poison gas, they will certainly be needed for decontamination.

The change in production priorities after the fall of France reflected a basic change in the chemical branch role from being prepared for gas warfare to providing supporting fire. There was more emphasis on their role of supporting an attack by firing rocket salvoes. As long as poison gas is not being used, Nebeltruppen will be employed for concentrated surprise fire against area targets. They will not be used for tasks which are the responsibility of the divisional artillery, nor are they able to put down defensive fire. The first mention that Nebeltruppen were interested in acquiring small half-tracks was recorded in a presentation by WaA In 9 to the A.H.A. department head on 4 June 1936:

Motorisation of the Nebeltruppen: The kl.gl.Zkw. (Lilliput off-road towing vehicle) should be tested. A single vehicle that could both contaminate and decontaminate would be ideal.

By July 1937, Büssing-NAG had received a contract for 300 transmissions with the drive shaft modified to provide power to auxiliary equipment such as the pumps and spreaders needed for contamination and decontamination vehicles. The vehicles in which these 300 transmissions were to be installed would have been ordered as well.

The trial Kleiner Entgiftungskraftwagen on a 0 Serie D 6 chassis.

The trial Kleiner Sprühkraftwagen based on a 0 Serie D 6 chassis.

Preliminary plans for unit organisation dated 23 October 1937 reveal that designs had been initiated for all three types of vehicles desired by the Nebeltruppen:

Gasspürer. auf Zkw.1t (poison gas detection section on 1-tonne half-track), *a kl.Entg.-Zkw.1t (Kleiner Entgiftungskraftwagen)* (small decontamination half-track), *and a kl.Sprüh.Zkw.1t (Kleiner Sprühkraftwagen)* (small poison gas sprayer half-track).

After an equipment demonstration in Ohrdruf on 11 May 1938, In 9 reported:

Because of production delays, the employment of an Abteilung to contaminate terrain will not be possible until March 1939. As notified by the Waffenamt, the last vehicles needed for terrain decontamination, the kl.Entg.Zgkw.1t (small decontamination half-tracks) *will arrive at the unit in February 1939.*

On 8 June 1938, In 9 informed the Allgemeines Heeresamt:

Troop trials should clarify if the previous use of 1t Zgkw. for contamination and decontamination can be replaced by 3t Zgkw. which have the following advantages: increased capability, a single type of vehicle in each Batterie, savings in the number of vehicles (eliminating the 1t Zgkw. für Gasspürer) and vehicle drivers. The advantages of the 1t Zgkw. in comparison to the 3t Zgkw. are: 10cm narrower and therefore easier to move on narrow trails and through forest; about 50cm lower and therefore easier to take cover in terrain and lower probability of being hit.

In 9 informed A.H.A. on 10 June 1938:

The Zgkw. for Gasspürer cannot be eliminated in the attempt to save on the number of vehicles. The replacement of the six le.Entg. und Verg. Zgkw. (1t) in every Batterie by two or at most four 3t Zgkw. will result in the same or increased capability of the Batterie and save two to four contamination and decontamination vehicles.

On 8 July 1938, In 9 reported on the future status of readiness of the Nebeltruppen:

The Vergiftungs-Batterien (poison gas contamination) cannot be employed until after 1 April 1939, because the full complement of Sprühfahrzeugen (spraying vehicles) will not be available until then.

On 27 October 1938, Waffenamt plans to cover the need for individual vehicle types to fill the last of the three peacetime Nebel-Abteilungen by March 1939 called for:

- 0% of the 1t l.Gasspür-Kw.10/1 by 15 November 1938, 67% by 31 December and 100% by 28 February 1939
- 66% of the 1t l.Entg.Kw. 10/2 by 15 November and 100% by 31 December 1938
- 0% of the 1t l.Sprüh.Kw. 10/3 by 15 November, 6% by 31 December 1938, and 100% by 28 February 1939

However, start-up of mass production of the le.Zgkw.1t Typ D 7 was significantly delayed due to continuous modifications. The 900 initially planned to be completed by the end of March 1939 were not all produced until August 1939. For example, Demag produced a le.Sprüh.Kw. (Sd. Kfz.10/3) with Fgst.Nr.100133 and Maybach NL 38 TRKM Motor Nr.52312 after July 1939.

A report dated 23 June 1939 on the requirements for Zugkraftwagen by the various branches for future army expansion reveals that the Sd.Kfz.10/2 and Sd.Kfz.10/3 had been eliminated and only the Sd.Kfz.10/1 remained. A total of 90 Sd.Kfz.10/1 were wanted by the Nebeltruppen; 36 to be completed by 1 April 1940, 36 by 1 October 1941, and 18 by 1 April 1942.

Due to the start of the war, the production program was accelerated, as revealed in the Zugkraftwagen production plans dated 20 December 1939:

90 Zgkw.1t Fgst. are urgently needed to produce 90 gas-detection vehicles. After these are completed, production at the rate of five chassis per month for Sd.Kfz.10/1 is sufficient.

On 3 May 1940, these plans were changed to:

After completing the 1000 Sfl. 2cm Flak 30 (Sd.Kfz.10/4) for the army, 30 Gasspürerkw. (Sd.Kfz.10/1) are to be produced each month until a total of 400 has been achieved, then continue at the rate of 10 per month.

For example, M.I.A.G. produced a Gasspürer-Kw. (Sd. Kfz.10/1) with Fgst.Nr.600063 and Maybach HL 42 TRKM Motor Nr.53199.

The last mention of production of the Gasspürerkw. (Sd.Kfz.10/1) for the Nebeltruppen is a report from 7 January 1943 that M.W.C. is to complete 10 D 7 with gas-detection provisions by 15 January 1943. Production of the Gasspürerkw. (Sd.Kfz.10/1) may have continued beyond this time, but it had definitely ceased by the end of 1943.

9.1 Gasspürerkraftwagen (Sd.Kfz.10/1)

As described in instruction manual H.Dv.210/2f, the Gasspürerkw. (poison gas detection vehicle) was outfitted with

Above: One of the first Gasspürerkraftwagen (Sd.Kfz.10/1) (poison gas detection vehicles), produced in 1938/early 1939, which had complex ventilation slits in the engine hood and did not have rails on the capped front and rear stowage bins. (NARA)
Below: A Gasspürerkraftwagen (Sd.Kfz.10/1) (poison gas detection vehicle) produced in 1939 with rails on the capped front and rear stowage bins and the original Äußeres Laufrad RS 2298 (outer roadwheel) and Inneres Laufrad RS 2192 (inner roadwheel). (NARA)

the following Gasspür and Gasabwehrmitteln (gas detection and protection equipment): 15 sets of le. Gasbekleidung (protective suits), two Gasanzeiger (gas indicators), 15 sets of Spürfähnchen (small flags), 12 Spürbüchsen (cans to carry detection powder), one Trommel Spürpulver 25 kg (drum with detection powder), two holders for Kampfstoffproben (poison gas samples), one Waffenentgiftungsmittel (weapon decontamination kit), one small shovel and one funnel to transfer the Spürpulver, one pair of gloves for the vehicle driver, and eight clothing bags.

The Spürgruppe (track marking section) consisted of a Gruppenführer (section leader), six Gasspürern (K.1 to K.6), and the Kraftfahrer (driver). When detecting, K.1 and K.2 lying on the fenders of the Gasspürer-Kw. dispensed Spürpulver to create a marked track. The detection powder reacted with any poison gas present by changing colour. K.3 through K.6 were dropped off at intervals to follow the vehicle and evaluate the presence of poison gas. The beginning of their sectors were marked with a cross composed of detection powder. When poison gas was found, the start was marked with a curved line of detection powder across the track, and the end of the contaminated sector marked with a straight line of detection powder across the track.

9.2 leichter Entgiftungskraftwagen (Sd.Kfz.10/2) D 7s

A description and operational guidance for the leichter Entgiftungskraftwagen (Sd.Kfz.10/2) (Bauart 1939) was published in manual D1119/2, dated 15 October 1941, as follows:

The leichte Entgiftungskraftwagen is a light off-road Zgkw.1t (D 7 chassis) with an upper body designed to spread decontamination chemicals in a 1-metre-wide strip and can also tow a trailer. Its characteristics different from a normal le.Zgkw.1t (Sd.Kfz.10) are:

Range on roads	250 km
Fuel capacity	86 litres
Highest speed while spreading	10 km/hr off-road
	20 km/hr on-road
Length	4.83 m
Width	1.90 m
Height with cover up	1.95 m
Height with cover down	1.70 m
Fording depth	65cm
Vehicle weight unladen	3890 kg
Load	880 kg
Maximum weight allowed	4900 kg

The Entgiftungs-Stoff (decontamination chemical) is stored in eight drums weighing a total of 480 kg (400 kg net weight). 200 kg can be loaded into the Streukasten (spreader bin). One drum with 50 kg can cover an area 1 metre wide by 160 metres long. The entire load of 400 kg will cover a 1300-metre-long strip.

The chassis is a standard 1t Zgkw.-Fahrgestell, Bauart D 7 in which an auxiliary drive has been installed for the spreader. Other changes include: Two fuel tanks behind the front seats. The left fuel tank has a tunnel for the spreader drive shaft. The Zughaken (towing pintle) for trailers is removable and when not

A leichter Entgiftungskraftwagen (Sd.Kfz.10/2). A special transfer box attached to the gearbox was located under the driver's seat and a drive shaft was connected to the left side of the Streuvorrichtung. Identified D 7k chassis were supplied by Adlerwerke. (WA)

Only about 60 to 70 leichte Entgiftungskraftwagen (Sd.Kfz.10/2) were produced in 1938/1939. They had a total of eight drums (200 kg decontaminant) stowed on side platforms with guard rails and a Streuvorrichtung (spreader) mounted on the rear. It featured a crew of four: the driver and co-driver at the front and two operators seated between the drums. This example is fitted with Zgw.51/240/160 cast track. (NARA)

Leichter Sprühkraftwagen
(Sd.Kfz.10/3)
mit Fahrgestell des le.Zgkw 1 t

About 67 leichte Sprühkraftwagen (Sd.Kfz.10/3) (poison gas sprayer vehicles) were produced in 1938/1939. The centre picture shows the 500 litre poison gas tank with the spraying mechanism mounted and pipework attached. The photo on the right shows the same leichter Sprühkraftwagen prepared for travel with the spraying mechanism stowed and canvas covers in place. (NARA)

in use should be stowed with the vehicle's tools.

The upper body consists of a Plattform-aufbau (platform) and a Streuvorrichtung (spreader), both made out of metal. It is covered completely by a canvas top that is fastened at the front on the windscreen and supported by three Spriegel (bows). The canvas sides by the driver and co-driver can be rolled up.

A load platform with collapsible outer rails is mounted above the right and left tracks. Four drums are stored and secured in place on each platform. At the same height as the platform, a Sitzbank (bench seat) for two crew members is located in front of the rear chassis wall. Just like the driver's and co-driver's seats, this seat has a removable rubber cushion.

The spreader is made with a bin to hold 200 kg of Entgiftungsstoff. There are two smooth spreader rollers located inside at the bottom of the bin for spreading chemicals between them. A rubber sheet is fastened at the rear to prevent the wind from blowing away the chemicals before they fall to the ground. A screen is installed in the bin to retain large clumps.

The spreader is powered from the left drive shaft through a differential, a clutch, another drive shaft, and a second differential to a chain drive connected by a chain to the drive chain for the spreader rollers. The clutch (Bauart Ortlinghaus, Type 2/205) along with the front differential is mounted in a housing on the left drive shaft. The shifting lever for the clutch is located to the right of the driver's seat.

The amount of chemicals spread is controlled by adjusting the distance between the two rollers. The adjusting device and lever with rest are mounted on the left side of the Streukasten. Depending on the moisture in the chemicals, the lever should be set normally at position 3 or 4 (out of a selection of 0 to 9) to spread the correct amount of 300 g/m². A second lever allows the spreader rollers to be opened wider.

The special tools for the spreader and the cover tarp are stowed in the tool bin on the right front fender, in another bin under the bench seat, and in holders. The Spriegel (bows) are stowed behind the driver's seat. The shovel, pick axe, long axe, and crow bar are stowed on the front fenders and on the Streukasten. The crew's baggage is stowed in a bin under the bench seat. The rifles are stowed in a rack behind the driver's seat.

9.3 leichter Sprühkraftwagen (Sd.Kfz.10/3) D 7k

The le.Sprühkw. (Sd.Kfz.10/3) was designed to provide Geländeverstärkungen (terrain reinforcement). The Behälter (tank) held 500 litres of liquid chemicals weighing about 650 kg. The liquid was sprayed using compressed air at only 1 atmospheric pressure from a Knorr V 50/220 driven by

pulleys and a drive belt. A 16-metre-wide zone was achieved by swinging the spray nozzle with a Schwenkvorrichtung (traversing device). The density laid down depended on the Schwenkvorrichtung setting and the vehicle speed.

On 15 April 1942, O.K.H./A.H.A./In 9 ordered the Sd.Kfz.10/3 to be converted for towing a 3.7cm Pak, as follows:

The 65 le.Sprühkw. (Sd.Kfz.10/3) on hand at the Heereszeugamt Hannover are to be outfitted for towing a 3.7cm Pak. The necessary wooden upper bodies and the two already completed Musterfahrzeuge (prototypes) are to be sent by rail to the H.Za. Hannover from the firm of D.W.M., Berlin-Borsigwalde. After receipt of the technical details, the work is to be rapidly accomplished, because the converted vehicles are intended for refurbishing Nebeltruppe field units. 216 rounds of Pak ammunition are stored in two ammunition bins that are mounted above the track guards. After conversion, these special-purpose vehicles are no longer usable as Sprühkw. The sprayer equipment will be disabled by taking out the pulley belts between the engine and the air compressor.

9.4 Organisation

On 23 October 1937, plans were made for organising Nebeltruppen units. Each Engifting-Batterie (mot) was to have six Gasspürgr. auf je kl.Zkw. (1t) and six kl.Entg.-Zkw. (1t). A Nebel-Gerät-Kolonne, the cover name for a Gelände-Vergiftungs-Kolonne (terrain contamination train), had 18 kl.Sprüh-Kw. (1t). During poison gas dispersal operations, these were to be exchanged for the decontamination vehicles in three batteries in the Entgiftungs-Abteilung (mot).

In a training manual for the Nebeltruppe dated 21 October 1939, the Entgiftungs-Abteilung (mot) was to have an Entgiftungs-Batterie with six Sd.Kfz.10/1 each manned by a driver, section leaders and six soldiers. The battalion also had 12 Sd.Kfz.11/2.

The following K.St.N. for the Nebeltruppen had one or more Sd.Kfz.10/1, 10/2, or 10/3. In some cases, they were substitutes or left over in units organised under earlier K.St.N. (or K.St.N. amendment orders):

- **Entgiftungs-Batterie (mot) (K.St.N.612), dated 1 October 1937**, was organised with six Gasspürer-Kw. (Sd.Kfz. 10/1), six le. Entgiftungs-Kw. (Sd.Kfz.10/2) and six m.Entgiftungs-Kw. (Sd.Kfz.11/2). As specified in the Army Mobilisation Plan dated 1 July 1938, if the unit had not received all of its vehicles when activated for war, an additional two Sd.Kfz.11/2 were to be used as substitutes for the six Sd.Kfz.10/2 and two Sd.Kfz.11/1were to be used as substitutes for the six Sd.Kfz.10/1.

- **Nebel-Werfer-Batterie (mot) K.St.N.614, dated 1 November 1939**, was organised with 12 Sd.Kfz.11/1. However, an official amendment dated 8 April 1940 was announced in the A.H.M. for this K.St.N to be altered with six Sd.Kfz.10/1 issued to the Munitions-Staffel (ammunition section), instead of six Sd.Kfz.11/1.
- **Nebel-Werfer-Batterie (mot) K.St.N.614, dated 1 February 1941**, with 10cm Nebelwerfer 40 authorised four Sd.Kfz.10/1 with special-purpose superstructures for the Munitions-Staffel as substitutes for four Sd.Kfz.11/4.
- **Entgiftungs-Batterie (mot) K.St.N.615, dated 1 November 1939**, was organised with six Gaspürerkraftwagen (Sd.Kfz.10/1) and 12 Sd.Kfz.11/2. However, le. Entgiftungskraftwagen (Sd.Kfz.10/2) had been ordered, produced, and issued to at least the first three Entgiftungs-Abteilungen; and these were retained by the units as a substitute for Sd.Kfz.11/2. On 15 April 1940, for example, the 2.Bttr./Entg.Abt.102 organised in accordance with K.St.N.615 dated 1Nov39, reported a strength of six Gaspürerkraftwagen (Sd.Kfz.10/1), seven le.Entgiftungskraftwagen (Sd.Kfz.10/2), and five m.Entgiftungskraftwagen (Sd.Kfz.11/2).
- **Schwere Werferbatterie (mot) K.St.N.615, dated 1 November 1941** with six 28/32cm Nebelwerfer 41 had seven Gaspürerkraftwagen (Sd.Kfz.10/1), six to tow the 28/32cm Nebelwerfer 41 and the seventh for the platoon leader of the 2nd Platoon to tow a Pak.
- **Werferbatterie (mot) K.St.N.617, dated 1 November 1941** with six 15cm Nebelwerfer 41 had only one Gaspürerkraftwagen (Sd.Kfz.10/1) für 3.7cm Pak for the platoon leader of the 2nd Platoon.
- **Leichte Entgiftungs-Gerät-Kolonne (mot) K.St.N.666, dated 1 November 1939** was organised with 18 m.Sprühkraftwagen (Sd.Kfz.11/3). However, le.Sprühkraftwagen (Sd.Kfz.10/3) had been produced, and issued to at least the first three Entgiftungs-Abteilungen, and these were retained by the units as a substitute for Sd.Kfz.11/3. As before, the le.Entg.-Ger.Kol/Entg. Abt.102 organised in accordance with K.St.N.666 dated 1 November 1939, had 12 le.Sprühkraftwagen (Sd. Kfz.10/3) and 18 m.Sprühkraftwagen (Sd.Kfz.11/3).
- **Stab einer Straßen-Entgiftungs-Abteilung (mot) K.St.N.609, dated 1 May 1941** was authorised to have two Gaspürerkraftwagen (Sd.Kfz.10/1) for the Gefechtsstab.
- **Straßen-Entgiftungs-Kompanie (mot) K.St.N.619, dated 1 February 1941** was authorised to have two Gaspürerkraftwagen (Sd.Kfz.10/1) and three le.Entgiftungskraftwagen (Sd.Kfz.10/2).

9.4.1 Orders to Create and Organise Units

A K.St.N. only specifies how a unit is to be organised.

For a K.St.N. to be applied, implementation orders were written by the O.K.H./Chef H Rüst u. BdE or O.K.H./Gen.St.d.H./Organisations-Abteilung. The following are examples of several O.K.H. orders for creating and organising Nebeltruppen units, as well as amending the K.St.N.

On 30 November 1939, the Chef H Rüst u. BdE ordered Nebelabteilung 5 to be reorganised into Nebelwerferabteilung 5 and Entgiftungsabteilung 5. The Nebelwerfer-Abteilungen for firing (gas and) Nebel were to be organised in accordance with K.St.N.604 for the Stab, K.St.N.614 for the three Nebelwerfer batteries, and K.St.N.664 for the le.Nebelwerferkolonne. The excess 18 medium decontamination vehicles and 18 gas detection vehicles were to be sent to Celle/Hannover for forming Entgiftungsabteilung 5 organised in accordance with K.St.N.604 for the Stab, K.St.N.615 for the three decontamination batteries, K.St.N.665 for a light decontamination train, and K.St.N.666 for an light decontamination equipment train.

On 29 April 1941, the O.K.H., Chef H Rüst u. BdE/A.H.A. ordered the activation of the Nebel-Lehr-Regiment to be sent to the front, organised as follows:

- K.St.N.601 v.1Feb41 - Rgt.Stb.Nbl.Tr.
- K.St.N.604 v.1Feb41 - I.Abt. Stb.Nbl.Werf.Abt.(mot)
- K.St.N.614 v.1Feb41 - two Nbl.Werf.Battr.(mot)
- K.St.N.664 v.1Feb41 - le.Nbl.Werf.Kol.(mot)
- K.St.N.607 v.1Feb41 - III.Abt. Stb.Nbl.Werf.Abt.d(mot)
- K.St.N.617 v.1Feb41 - three Nbl.Werf.Battr.d (mot)
- K.St.N.667 v.1Feb41 - le.Nbl.Werf.Kol.d (mot)

K.St.N.617 was authorised at full strength with eight Werfer per Batterie. The I.Abteilung was outfitted with Nebelwerfer 40 and the III.Abteilung with Nebelwerfer d.

On 17 October 1941, O.K.H. ordered the creation of Nebelwerfer-Batterie d (mot) 151 on 20 October at Celle to be sent to Panzergruppe Afrika; organised in accordance with K.St.N. 617 Nbl.Werfer-Battr. d (mot), as amended on 2 May 1941 to reduce the number of Nebelwerfer from 8 to 6. In addition, the Batterie was to receive a Sd.Kfz.10/1 for the platoon leader of the 2nd Platoon (instead of a Kfz.1) and a Pak in accordance with a further amendment to K.St.N.617, as ordered by the Gen StdH/Org.Abt. on 18 September 1941.0

9.4.2 Nebelwerfer Units

In a report prepared by O.K.H./A.H.A./ In 9 on 24 February 1938, the Ob.d.H., Generaloberst von Brauchitsch (Commander-in-Chief) was informed that previously Nebel-Abteilungen 1 und 2 (Königsbrück und Bremen) and Nebel-Lehr- und Versuchsabteilung (Celle) had been formed, each with three Batterien with 8 Nebelwerfer per battery. It was planned to form a new unit with vehicles for terrain decontamination and contamination with poison gas after the Summer of 1938. Nebel-Abteilung 5 (Horb) was to be formed in the Autumn of 1938, and two additional Nebel-Abteilungen each Autumn in 1939, 1940, and 1941, for a total of 10. The General Staff of the Army had ordered that the Nebeltruppe be organised so that every Abteilung could fire smoke screens and poison gas and contaminate the terrain with Sprühfahrzeuge.

On 23 May 1938, O.K.H./A.H.A./In 9 proposed that when each peacetime Nebel-Abteilung was mobilised for war, it would be reorganised to create a Nebel-Werfer Abteilung (for firing smoke screens and poison gas) and an Entgiftungs-Abteilung, which also had equipment for contaminating terrain.

The O.K.H. Gliederung (organisation charts), dated 15 January 1940, reveal that five Nebel-Werfer-Abteilungen (1, 2, 3, 4 (on 1 February 1940) and 5) had been created, each with three Nebel-Werfer-Batterien and a le.Neb.Werf.Kol. as well as three Entgiftungs-Abteilungen (101, 102, and 105) each with three decontamination batteries, a le.Entgiftung Kol., and a le.Entgiftung Ger.Kol.

On 15 April 1940, Entgiftungs-Abteilung 102 reported having on hand 18 Gasspür-Kw. (1t) (Sd.Kfz.10/1), 22 le.Entgiftungs-Kw. (1t) (Sd.Kfz.10/2), and 12 le.Sprüh-Kw. (1t) (Sd.Kfz.10/3).

The O.K.H. organisation charts dated 1 February 1941 show that the Nebeltruppen had been expanded to:

- Nine Nebel-Werfer-Abteilungen (1, 2, 3, 4, 5, 6, 7, 8 (with s.Wurfgerät), and 9), each with three Nebel-Werfer-Batterien and a le.Neb.Werf.Kol.
- Three Nebel-Werfer-Regimenter d (51, 52, and 53) each with three (I., II., and III.) Nebel-Werfer d Abteilungen each with three Nebel-Werfer d Batterien and a le.Neb.Werf.Kol.
- Five Entgiftungs-Abteilungen (101, 102, 103, 104, and 105), each with three Entgiftung Batterien and a le.Entgiftung Kol.

As ordered on 25 February 1941, Nebel-Werfer Abteilung 1 and 7 were converted into the I. and II.Abt./Nebel-Werfer-Regiment 54.

Three Straßen-Entgiftungs-Abteilungen (131, 132, and 133), each with three roadway decontamination batteries, were created by orders dated 5 March 1941. All three Straßen-Entgiftungs-Abteilungen and five Entgiftung-Abteilung were converted into Abteilungen with 28/32cm Nebelwerfer 41.

Additional Nebeltruppen units and their organisations are covered in Panzer Tracts No.22-2.

A re-purposed leichter Entgiftungskraftwagen (Sd.Kfz.10/2) towing a 15cm Nebelwerfer 41. It retains side platforms but has had the spreader removed. In addition, crew seats and a wooden storage unit have been added. (Bundesarchiv Bild 146-1978-078-07)

Above: This Gasspürerkraftwagen (Sd.Kfz.10/1) (poison gas detection vehicle) completed by Büssing-NAG in 1939 or early 1940 was outfitted with a larger stowage bin in the crew compartment. (WA)

Right: This Gasspürerkraftwagen (Sd.Kfz.10/1) completed in 1939 or early 1940 has the standard capped front and rear stowage bins but with rails added. (WA)

A Gasspürerkraftwagen (Sd.Kfz.10/1) on a Ausf.B chassis assigned to the 6./schweres Werfer-Regiment 1 being used to tow a 28cm Nebelwerfer 41. (Bundesarchiv Bild 101I-049-0176-15 & 16)

Above: The 6./schweres Werfer-Regiment 1 moves off with three Gasspürerkraftwagen (Sd.Kfz.10/1) assigned to tow 28cm Nebelwerfer 41. (Bundesarchiv Bild 101I-49-176-26)

Below: A Gasspürerkraftwagen (Sd.Kfz.10/1) with the strengthened A-Rad AS5114 outer roadwheels and I-Rad und Leitrad 021B 2685 U9 inner roadwheels and idler wheel completed by M.I.A.G in 1940. (Bundesarchiv Bild L 25688)

The reliability and longevity of the D 7 is demonstrated by this leichter Sprühkraftwagen (Sd.Kfz.10/3) with the 500 litre Behälter (tank) removed. It is being used to tow a 15cm Nebelwerfer 41 at the cessation of hostilities in May 1945 in the town of Hradec Kralove. (HK)

11. Selbstfahrlafette (Sd.Kfz.10/4) für 2cm Flak 30
Selbstfahrlafette (Sd.Kfz.10/5) für 2cm Flak 38

The concept and tactical value of a 2cm Flak on a self-propelled half-track were already considered in a report entitled Offensive Abwehr Panzerwagen (Offensive Defence Against Armour) by the WaA/WaA Prüf on 30 October 1935, as follows:

***2cm Flak auf Selbstfahrlafette (l.gl.Zkw.) (2cm anti-aircraft gun on a self-propelled carriage, the 1 ton Zugkraftwagen).** A gun has been developed for the Luftschutztruppen (air-defence forces). When firing Panzergranate (armour-piercing rounds), it can penetrate 12mm of armour at 700m at a striking angle of 30°. Due to its higher muzzle velocity, it has somewhat better penetration capability than the 2cm gun mounted in the La.S.100 (Pz.Kpfw. II) and schweren Panzerspähwagen (heavy armoured cars). In comparison to the La.S.100, the 2cm Flak auf Selbstfahrlafette has the advantages of a substantially higher road speed, somewhat better terrain crossing ability and off-road speed.*

In comparison to the more numerous Tak in the Panzerwagenabwehr (anti-tank units). This is due to its its practical rate of fire of 14 to 16 rounds per minute and the fact that the 2cm Flak 30 has the choice of single-shot or automatic fire (cyclic rate of fire of 280 rounds per minute, practical 120) is favourably valued. Practical comparison trials have been initiated to determine if this postulation is correct.

Finally, by employing both Panzergranaten and Sprenggranaten (high explosive) ammunition, this weapon can be selectively employed as both a anti-tank and anti-aircraft weapon, a large advantage for this weapon. This one gun can provide Truppenluftschutz (local air defence), defend marching columns against surprise attacks from tank units and, to a limited extent, participate in offensively fighting tanks.

A disadvantage is the relatively high profile, the lack of an armour shield (associated with its present use only as a Flak), and the impossibility of rapidly mounting and dismounting the gun from the carriage due to its present design. It takes about 5 to 10 minutes to mount and dismount the gun from the carriage.

Up to now, a trial vehicle has been completed that is exclusively intended for use as a Flak with 360° traverse. The firing height is about 2 metres.

An Aufbau (upper body) for a kl.gl.Zkw. (3 ton Zugkraftwagen) is now being developed with a firing height of only 1.70 metres. This is also intended only for Flugabwehr (anti-aircraft defence) but is completely usable as a Tak auf Selbstfahrlafette (self-propelled anti-tank gun).

Further development led to the design and testing of a Selbstfahrlafette 2cm Flak on the smallest of the Zugkraftwagen series, code named Lilliput. Both the D ll 3 and D 6 chassis were used to create a few experimental vehicles for trials and troop testing.

10.1 Description

The 2cm Flak 30 was mounted on a Sonderaufbau AS 5304 (special upper body) designed for the Selbstfahrlafette 2cm Flak. The weight of the gun and crew was supported by a complex rigid frame secured to the top of the D 7 hull. The sides with curved corner folding sections and the tail gate were attached to the frame so that they could be folded down horizontally to extend the sides and rear of the platform. Ten Munitionskästen (ready bins for one Magazine 32 or 38 with 20 rounds) were secured onto the outside of the folding sides and rear. An additional Magazinkasten 30 located beside the co-driver held two Magazine 32 or 38 for a total of 40 rounds.

The frame was covered by a sheet metal platform with hatches for access into the interior and four Sitzklappen (folding seats with seat cushions - two at the front and two at the rear) for the gun crew. The 2cm Flak 30 carriage was secured by two Lagerungen (mountings) at the front and a Halterung (holder with a crossbar) at the rear. Three Lager (disc mounts) bolted to the platform were used as rests for the 2cm Flak 30 levelling pads (spaced 920mm apart side to side and also 920mm apart from front to rear).

The normal Kotflügel 021 B 26867 (fender) was replaced with the AS 5205/6 for the Sfl. 2cm Flak (at Demag starting with Fgst.Nr.100101 and by Adler for all their Sfl. 2cm Flak) This change to the fenders was associated with relocating the Halter für Fahrtrichtungsanzeiger und Rückblickspiegel AS 5373/4 (mount for the turn signals and rear-view mirror) for the Sfl. 2cm Flak. There were also two Begrenzungsanzeiger AS 5265 (width markers) mounted on the fenders.

The Selbstfahrlafette 2cm Flak was about 4.75 metres long, 2.02 (later 2.156) metres wide, and 2.20 (later 2.00) metres high, and had an empty weight of 4075 kg. It towed a Sonder-Anhänger 51 (special-pupose single axle trailer) on which was mounted a Zübehor und Munitionskasten (accessory and ammunition bin). These were for stowing an additional 640 rounds of 2cm ammunition in magazines and boxes holding the Linealvisiere and Flakvisier 35 (gun sights) and the Em 1 m R (rangefinder).

10.2 Production

Assembly of 195 Truppenluftschutz 2cm Flak auf Zgkw.1t for the Heer (army) and 175 for the Luftwaffe was demanded on short notice, with contracts awarded in May 1939. On 5 July 1939, Wa J Rü 2 informed Wa J Rü on the status of Truppenluftschutz 2cm Flak auf Zgkw.1t production:

The requirement from A.H.A./In 6 that 62 Zgkw. 1t mit Aufbauten für 2cm Flak be delivered by 10 July 1939 cannot be met because of the short deadline. Delivery of a total of 70 will occur during the period from 18 to 24 July 1939. However, the final deadline for delivery of all 195 by 1 August 1939 will be met.

In its monthly report for production in July 1939, Wa J Rü noted that:

195 Aufbauten auf 1t Zgkw. Fgst. f. 2cm Flak 30 were completed for the Heer (63 Aufbauten could not be mounted because Fahrgestell were not available) and 175 for the Luftwaffe. The orders have been completed.

In the future plans for Zugkraftwagen production (20 December 1939), it was noted that from the overall Zgkw.1t production, the Heer needed a total of 1000 Zgkw. f. Sfl. 2cm Flak 30 by 31 March 1940. The 195 previously completed for the Heer counted against this total. After this order was completed, production was to continue at the rate of 25 per month. On 22 February 1940, a note was added that in addition to those already ordered for the Heer, another 304 (Sd.Kfz.10/4) were needed for the Luftwaffe by 20 June 1940. The production schedule was again altered on 3 May 1940:

After completion of the 1000 Sfl. 2cm Flak 30 (Sd.Kfz.10/4) for the Heer, continue production at the rate of about 45 Sfl. 2cm Flak 30 (Sd.Kfz.10/4) per month for the Luftwaffe until the ordered 304 are delivered, then continue at the rate of 25 Sd.Kfz.10/4 per month.

The actual production for the Heer and Luftwaffe was reported as:

A trial Selbstfahrlafetten 2cm Flak 30 on the 0 Serie D 6 chassis. It is equipped with Auffahrschienen on a holder at the front and Seilrollen (cable pulleys) on both sides. The latter acted as pulleys for hauling the 2cm Flak 30 on and off the Sfl. (AT)

Left: A trial Selbstfahrlafetten 2cm Flak 30 on the 0 Serie D 6 chassis equipped with Auffahrschienen now carried on a holder at the front and Seilrolle (cable rollers) on both sides, which acted as pulleys for hauling the 2cm Flak 30 on and off the Sfl. (AT)

Below: A production Demag D6 chassis used to create a Selbstfahrlafette für 2cm Flak 30 mit Auffahrschienen. (HLD)

As notes on 1t Zgkw. production, Wa J Rü reported 30 Fg. f. Tr.L.S. were completed in January 1940, 190 in February, 299 in March, 294 in April, and 114 in May for a total of 927 chassis. Adlerwerke completed 350 Sfl. 2cm Flak (with Fgst.Nr. 200905 to 201254) from February to May 1940.

The Heer reported production of completed 2cm Flak Tr.L.S. auf Sfl. 1t Zgkw., as follows:

January 1940. 1000 ordered for the Heer cannot be reported until in February, because reports have not arrived from the H.Abn.Stellen.
April 1940. Goal: 354, actually completed: 301.
May 1940. Goal: 22, actually completed: 66. The contract is fulfilled. There are no further orders.

The Luftwaffe independently reported production of the completed 2cm Flak Truppenluftschutz auf Sonderfahrlafette 1t Zgkw. for them, as follows:

January 1940. 275 ordered for the Luftwaffe, scheduled at 50 Aufbauten auf 1t Zgkw. für 2cm Flak 30 per month from January to March 1940. Aufbauten for the 2cm Tr.L.Sch. will first be delivered in February.
February 1940. 47 2cm Flak Truppenluftschutz auf Sfl. 1t Zgkw. completed.
March 1940. 100 2cm Flak TrL.S auf Sfl. 1t Zgkw. completed
April 1940. 0 completed; 100 have already been produced. No new contracts.
May-July 1940. 0 completed.
August 1940. 6 completed for a total of 106. No further orders.

On 15 July 1940, Reichsminister der Luftwaffe and Oberfbefehlshaber der Luftwaffe (Reich Minister for the Air Force and Commander-in-Chief of the Air Force) reported the status of Selbstfahrlafetten (Sd.Kfz.10/4) production:

In response to an order from L.E.3 dated 11 May 1939, L.E.4 I requisitioned 400 Aufbauten f. Sfl. 2cm Flak auf Zgkw. 1t. To fill this order Wa J Rü awarded contracts for Aufbauten (upper bodies) with the following assembly plants:

175	Wumag, Görlitz, Auftrag 2-VIII-172-9001/39L
20	Wumag, Görlitz, Auftrag 2-VIII-172-9002/39L
35	Dürkopp-Werke, Bielefeld, Auftrag 2-VIII-172-9003/39L
35	Eisenwerk Weserhuette, Bad Oeynhausen, Auftrag 2-VIII-172-9004/39L
35	Benteler-Werke, Bielefeld, Auftrag 2-VIII-172-9005/39L
100	Wumag, Görlitz, Auftrag 2-VIII-172-9015/39L

Contract no.2-VII-172-9012/38L was issued to Wumag, Görlitz. Based on reports from Wa J Rü (WuG2 VIII), all of these contracts had been completed.

As had been planned in May 1940, production of the 2cm Flak Truppenluftschutz auf Sonderfahrlafette 1t Zgkw continued at a lower rate per month starting in the Autumn of 1940. In its monthly reports under 1t Zgkw. production Wa J Rü noted that 67 Fgst. T.L.S were completed in September 1940, 23 Fg. f. T.L.S. in October, 1 Fgst. and 20 as Sd.Kfz.10/4 in November 1940. No further notes on 2cm Flak T.L.S. auf Sfl. 1t Zgkw. were made in the Wa J Rü reports from December 1940 to September 1944.

In the Heeres Panzerprogramm 1941 (5-year production plans for the next five years) dated 30 May 1941, the Heereswaffenamt reported that the Heer needed 5040 Sfl. 2cm Flak and the Luftwaffe 1750 vehicles. Even though there was no requirement for additional Sd.Kfz.10/4, production of these was planned to continue at the rate of about 50 per month until the start-up of Sfl. 2cm Flak 38 auf Fgst.3t Zgkw production.

Even though they were not separately reported or noted by Wa J Rü in its monthly reports, production of the Sfl. 2cm Flak (Sd.Kfz.10/4) had actually continued. Adlerwerke reported that it had completed a total of 736 D 7 mit Sfl. Aufbau by 31 December 1941 and still had 318 left in its contract, of which 18 were scheduled to be completed in January 1942. The total of 736 includes an unknown number produced by Adlerwerke in July 1939, 350 completed from February to May 1940 (Fgst.Nr. 200905 to 201254) and the rest at a rate of about 25 per month starting in the Autumn of 1940. By the end of 1942, Adlerwerke had completed another 273 D 7 mit Sfl.Aufbau for a total of 1009 and were scheduled to complete the remainder of their contract for 1054 in January (25) and February (last 20) 1943.

Mechanische Werke Cottbus was awarded contract 213-0025/41H, which included 75 Sd.Kfz.10/5 that were completed by the end of 1943 and a second contract 213-0025/41H for 900 Sd.Kfz.10/5, of which 200 were completed by the end of 1943 and 687 in 1944. The last 13 were completed as Sd.Kfz.10 in 1944.

10.3 Modifications Introduced During Production

10.3.1 2cm Flak 30 Schutzschild (Gun Shield)

Some of the 2cm Flak 30 mounted on the Sfl. (Sd. Kfz.10/4) produced in 1939 and 1940 had a Schutzschild (gun shield) and others did not. On 19 July 1940, A.H.A./In 2 announced a modification to reposition the 2cm Flak 30 Schutzschild 135mm higher.

Above: Three new Sfl. (Sd.Kfz.10/4) für 2cm Flak 30 on the road between Haarlem and Amsterdam on 17 May 1940. (PW)
Below: The Demag D7 chassis was used to create the first series of 370 Sd.Kfz.10/4 in 1939. Prior to the mounting of the 2cm Flak 30, one can see how the carriage was secured to the special platform by two Lagerung (mountings) at the front and a single Halterung (holder with crossbar) at the rear. Each was provided with a ratchet system for raising and lowering to adjust the level of the gun. The four hatches opened to provide access to storage and seats for four crew members. The backrest cushions of these seats can be seen hanging off the platform sides. (HLD)

Above: Originally each Fla-Kompanie (mot S) was outfitted with 18 Sd.Kfz.10/4 of which 12 had 2cm Flak 30 mounted and the other six were used for ammunition carriers, like this one completed by Demag in 1939. (HLD)
Below: The side view shows the extent of the canvas cover on the same 1939 Demag Sfl. (HLD)

Above: A 1939 Sd.Kfz.10/4. The 2cm Flak 30 has been back-fitted with an armour shield. (Bundesarchiv Bild 101I-251-965-15a)
Below: The second series of Sd.Kfz.10/4 für 2cm Flak 30 appeared in 1940. They were completed with Karabiner-Halterung AS5290/4 (holders for six 98k rifles) mounted on the left and right fenders. That was followed by the fitting of Auffahrschienen and Seilrollen. This D 7 chassis was completed by Büssing-NAG. (CM)

The part AS 5290/4 for six 98k rifles were mounted on the left and right fenders starting in 1940. A sheet metal cover over the rifle racks was added in 1942.

10.3.2 Selbstfahrlafette (Sd.Kfz.10/4) für 2cm Flak 30 (mit Auffahrschienen) (Loading Ramps)

In order to dismount the 2cm Flak 30 from the vehicle and employ it on the ground in a concealed position, Selbstfahrlafette (Sd.Kfz.10/4) Baujahr 1940 were outfitted with Auffahrschienen that were stowed in a Befestigung AS 5245/1+2 (mount) on the front. A Plattform-Abschluss AS 5237 frame mounted at the front of the platform had Seilrollen (cable rollers) on both sides, which served to assist hauling or lowering the 2cm Flak 30 mounted on the Sd.Ah.51 (special trailer) up the loading ramps. For this operation, the loading ramps were secured into two slots on the top edge of the lowered Rückwandklappe AS 5211 (tail gate). To compensate for the additional weight and stress that occurred while loading and unloading the 2cm Flak on the Sd.Ah.51, triangular supports were added to the back of the tail gate that acted as support braces and two Langsholm AS 5238 metal beam extensions were added to the hull sides to support the platform at the rear. According to D672/4, the loading ramps (and associated accessories, such as the cable pulleys on the platform frame and mount on the front of the vehicle) were no longer installed after Baujahr 1941.

10.3.3 2cm Flak 38

The 2cm Flak 38 was already accepted as standard equipment on 5 January 1939. However, the 2cm Flak 30 continued in production. Production records only reported a total number of 2cm Flak completed each month, not broken down by model. The 2cm Flak 30 continued to be mounted on the Selbstfahrlafette (Sd.Kfz.10/4) until 1943, being gradually replaced by the 2cm Flak 38 starting in 1941. The levelling pads on a 2cm Flak 38 were much farther apart than those on a 2cm Flak 30; therefore, the 2cm Flak 38 could not be readily mounted on a (Sd.Kfz.10/4) outfitted for a 2cm Flak 30, and vice versa. Initially, the 2cm Flak 38 were mounted on Selbstfahrlafette (Sd.Kfz.10/4) mit Auffahrschienen which still had a 1.89-metre-wide platform designed for the 2cm Flak 30.

10.3.4 Selbstfahrlafette (Sd.Kfz.10/5) für 2cm Flak 38

Starting in 1942, the supporting frame and platform were widened to 2.245 metres to provide more space for the Flak 38 with its levelling pads spaced 1.52 metres apart side to side and 1.76 metres apart from front to rear. The Plattform-Abschluss (rails) mounted at the front of the platform reverted to the original design from 1939. The outer edge of the track guard was angled outward to match the wider platform. Even with the wider platform, the vehicle was still known as the Selbstfahrlafette (Sd.Kfz.10/4) für 2cm Flak 38. The earliest document found with the name changed to Selbstfahrlafette (Sd.Kfz.10/5) für 2cm Flak 38 is dated 1 October 1943. Despite that, the name Selbstfahrlafette (Sd.Kfz.10/4) with a 2cm Flak 38/3 was still used in a K.A.N. dated 1 December 1944.

10.3.5 Behelfspanzerung (Expedient Armour)

On 29 January 1943, Luftwaffe In 6 announced a modification to mount Behelfspanzerung to protect the driver, co-driver, and radiator of the le.Zgkw.1t (Sd.Kfz.10/4) als Selbstfahrlafette für 2cm Flak 30, für 2cm Flak 30 (mit Auffahrtschienen), and für 2cm Flak 38. This modification was to be accomplished by the Kfz. Werkstätten (unit workshops). The following armour components were needed to complete this modification: Windschutzpanzer (windscreen armour), rechter Seitenpanzer (right-side armour), linker Seitenpanzer (left-side armour), and Kühlerpanzer (radiator armour). This modification was to be completed after the components arrived. These armour components were to be issued on a case-by-case basis. The Sonderausschuss Panzerfertigung (Special Committee for Armour Production) reported that Poldihutte had produced 293 sets of armour plates for the 1t Zgkw. in 1943; 61 in March, 28 in April, 95 in May, 56 in June, 16 in July, and 37 in August.

10.4 Organisation and Units

According to K.St.N. 192 dated 1 December 1939, a Flugabwehr-Kompanie with 12 2cm Flak 30 was organised with 18 Sfl. (Sd.Kfz.10/4) in three platoons, 12 with guns mounted and 6 for ammunition transport.

Fla-Kp.(mot S) K.St.N.192 dated 1 February 1941 had three platoons with a total of 18 Sfl. (Sd.Kfz.10/4), of which 12 had guns mounted. Alternately, it could have 12 Sfl. (Sd.Kfz.10/4) with towed 2cm Flak-Vierling 38 in the third platoon.

The above K.St.N.192 was amended as announced in the A.H.M. by A.H.A./In 2 on 7 February 1941:

The Flak companies with 2cm Flak 30 are to be issued only 15 (Sd.Kfz.10/4) instead of 18. When there are Flak-Vierling in the unit, only 10 Zgkw. (Sd.Kfz.10/4) are to be issued instead of 12. Each platoon is to have four (Sd.Kfz.10/4) with guns and one (Sd.Kfz.10/4) for Munitionstransport.

K.St.N.192 dated 1 November 1941 had two platoons

with a total of eight 2cm Flak mounted on eight (Sd.Kfz.10/4) plus two Sfl. (Sd.Kfz. 10/4) for ammunition transport.

Fla-Kp.(Sf.)(gek) K.St.N.192gek dated 1 June 1943 had three platoons with 18 Selbstfahrlafetten 1t (Sd.Kfz.10/4) with 12 2cm Flak 38. That K.St.N. was superseded by Fla-Kp.(12 Gesch. 2cm Flak Sf.) K.St.N.192 dated 1Apr44 for an organisation with twelve 2cm Flak 38 auf Selbstfahrlafetten 1t (Sd.Kfz.10/4).

K.St.N.2202 dated 1 November 1940 for a Luftwaffe 2cm Flak Battery (12 gun) was amended on 1 October 1943, reducing the total number of guns to 11. There were either 11 Sd.Kfz.10/4 or Sd.Kfz.10/5 in the unit, with a total of either nine Flak 30 or Flak 38 guns.

The Selbstfahrlafette (Sd.Kfz.10/4) with a 2cm Flak 30 or 38 was included in the K.St.N./K.A.N. for additional units, such as:

9 in Stbs.Kp.d s.Pz.Abt., K.St.N.1150d, 15Aug42
6 in Stbs.Kp.Pz.Abt. Panther, K.St.N.1150a, 10Jan43
9 in Stbs.Kp.b Pz.Abt., K.St.N.1150b, 25Jan43
8 in s.Kp.(mot) Ski-Jg.Rgt., K.St.N.187b, 1Jan45

The Selbstfahrlafette (Sd.Kfz.10/5) with a 2cm Flak 38 was listed in the K.St.N./K.A.N. for additional units, such as:

6 in s.Pz.Gr.Kp. K.St.N.1115(fG), 1Nov44
6 in s.Pz.Gr.Kp. K.St.N.1115, 1Apr45

10.4.1 Heeres Units from 1940 to 1942

The O.K.H. Gliederung (organisation charts) dated 1 April 1940, reveal that six Fla-Abt.(Sfl.) (numbered 601 through 606) and Fla.Kp.631 had been created with three Fla-Kp. each with 12 2cm Flak Sfl. In addition eight Fla-Btl. (mot) had been created, each with five or six Fla-Kp.(mot) each with twelve 2cm Flak, as follows: 1.-5.Kp./Fla-Btl.31, 1.-6.Kp./Fla-Btl.46, 1.-6.Kp./47, 1.-6.Kp./Fla-Btl.48, 1.-6. Kp./Fla-Btl.52, 1.-6.Kp./Fla-Btl.55, 1.-6.Kp./Fla-Btl.59, 1.-5.Kp./Fla-Btl.66. By November 1940, these independent companies were converted to Fla-M.G.Kp. (mot S), organised in accordance with K.St.N.192 dated 1 December 1939 and amended on February 1941.

Some of these independent companies were attached to Panzer-Divisions and Infanterie-Division (mot) prior to the campaign in the West in May/June1940. For example, the Fla-Kp. 2./59 was assigned to the 1.Pz.Div., 2./47 to the 2.Pz. Div., 6./59 to the 3.Pz.Div., 5./66 to the 4.Pz.Div., 2./55 to the 5.Pz.Div., 3./46 to the 6.Pz.Div., 3./59 to the 7.Pz.Div., 4./48 to the 8.Pz.Div., 3./47 to the 9.Pz.Div., and 3./55 to

the 10.Pz.Div.

Not only were these units intended for anti-aircraft defence, they were also used to provide ground support. On 20 April 1940, Fla-Abt.601 and Fla-Kp.6./46, 2./48, 1./52, 3./52, 6./52, 4./55, 6./59, and 5./66 were issued 480 Spr.Gr.Patr. Üb. (high-explosive training rounds) per company to practice Erdzielschiessen (firing at ground targets).

The Heeres Gliederung chart from November 1940 has three additional Fla-Abt.(Sfl.) numbered 607 to 609 that were formed from May to September 1940, too late for the campaign in the West. The next five Fla-Abt. (610, 611, 612, 613, and 615) were formed in January through April 1941 as motorised units with each company towing 12 2cm Flak. These were followed by the formation of Fla-Abt.(Sfl.) 614 and 616 in May 1941, 618 in November, and 619 in December 1941, each with three companies of 8 2cm Flak Sfl. and 2 towed 2cm Flakvierling 38.

Additional Fla-Kp. were assigned to the Panzer-Divisions and Infanterie-Division (mot) formed in 1940 to 1942, such as the 1.Kp./Fla.Abt.608 with Pz.Jg.Abt.61 in the 11.Pz.Div., 4./52 with Pz.Jg.Abt.2 in the 12.Pz.Div., 4./66 in the 13.Pz. Div., 2./608 in the 14.Pz.Div., 6./66 in the 16.Pz.Div., 1./66 in the 17.Pz.Div., 631.Fla.Kp. in the 18 Pz.Div., and the entire Fla.Abt.606 in the 5.le.Div. (renamed 21.Pz.Div.). As ordered by the GenStdH/Org.Abt.on 3 May 1942 (amended on 28 May 1942), the 2cm Fla-Kpn. were incorporated into schnelle Verbände (swift units):

Both Fla.Kp. already available in the Inf.Div.(mot) are to be incorporated into the Inf.Regt. as the 14.(Fla.Kp.). The Fla. Kp. in Pz.Div. remain with the Pz.Jäg.Abt. and retain their old designation. Previously independent Heeres-Fla.Kp. are to be incorporated as the 10.(Fla.Kp.) in Schützen-Regimenter of the 3., 9., 11., 13., 14., 16., 22., 23., and 24.Pz.Div. and the 14.(Fla.Kp.) in Inf.Regt. of the 3., 16., 29., and 60.Inf.Div. (mot). For example, the 5./31 became the 10.(Fla.Kp.)/S.R.21, and the 6./55 became the 10.(Fla.Kp.)/S.R.26 in the 24.Pz.Div.

As ordered on 9 March 1942, the 16.Kp./Inf.Rgt.GD1 and 2 in Inf.Div.Grossdeutschland were formed as Fla.Kp.(mot S) K.St.N.192 dated 1 February 1941 with eight 2cm Flak Sfl. (Sd.Kfz.10/4) and two towed 2cm Flak-Vierling 38.

10.4.2 Luftwaffe Units

The Luftwaffe had formed 23 le.Flak-Abt.(mot) and (Sf.) by 1 September 1939. There were eight le.Flak-Abt.(Sf.) with 22 Flakbattr. (2cm) on 1 December 1940 and 15 le.Flak-Abt. (Sf.) with 31 Flakbattr. (2cm) on 1 June 1941. The le.Flak-Abt.(Sf.) 71, 75, 77, 81, 82, 84, 91, 92, 93, 95, 96, 97, and 851 with nine or twelve 2cm Flak Sfl. (Sd.Kfz.10/4) in each of their 2. and 3.Batterie were listed as being available on 1 September 1943. In addition, the 4.Battr./Flak-Rgt. 'Hermann Göring' was reported as having 9 Sd.Kfz.10/4 on 20 October 1942.

10.5 Experience Reports

The following experience report on the 2cm Flak 30 Sfl. and the 2cm Flak 38 was written on 30 August 1942 by the Waffenamt liaison officer assigned to Panzerarmee Afrika:

The superiority of the German Zugkraftwagen is unsurpassed, even in the desert. The 1t Zgkw. is too weak to be used in Africa, because it is continuously overloaded. The lack of operational Zugkraftwagen is constantly very high. It is very susceptible to damage and needs many repairs. The major problem is the Gummipolster (rubber pads) that are extremely worn out due to the stony ground. It is proposed that the tracks be replaced with those without rubber. Due to the design of the vehicle, however, it is probably not possible without other design changes.

2cm Flak 30 Sfl. - Of all the 2cm Flak models, the Flak 30 Sfl. is liked the best. The Sfl. (1t gl.Zgkw.) is overloaded and often fails due to hits in the radiator.

There are no problems with the weapon, and it is highly valued. The Spr.Gr. (high-explosive rounds) have no effect against armoured aircraft. The troops solution is to fire a mixture of Pzgr. (armour-piercing) and Sprgr. No gun barrels on the 2cm Flak 30 have burst or swollen.

There is insufficient protection against dust. There should be a dust cover for the entire Flak 30.

Because of the Schutzschild (armour shield), which could be stronger, magazines cannot be loaded at all elevations. A modification is needed. The Visierblende (sight guard) is unusable because the gunner cannot aim with it in place. The Rohrblende (barrel guard) hinders the crew in quickly clearing stoppages. There is no protection against sand accumulating in the magazines.

The Linealvisiere (linear sights) are no longer available. They have been requisitioned. Replacement crews are no longer trained on the Linealvisier.

The pair of parallel mirrors in the Reflexvisier (reflection sight) has not worked out, because aircraft cannot be identified in strong sunlight. Blue glass is said to result in better recognition.

Sand gets into the Rechendosen (computing box) of the

A Selbstfahrlafette (Sd.Kfz.10/4) without the carrier brackets for loading ramps on the front undergoing engine maintenance. The canvas cover on the windscreen was to prevent damage when the gun was firing. (PW)

A section of a Wehrmacht Fla-Kompanie (mot S) maintain their Sfl. (Sd.Kfz.10/4) für 2cm Flak 30. The vehicle on the left appears to be from the 1939 production, while the rest have the racks for six 98k rifles and the equipment for dismounting the guns. The Flak guns have been fitted with the Schutzschild. (PW)

The seven-man crew prepare to dismount a 2cm Flak 30 using the unfolded Auffahrschienen (loading ramps). (PW)

A disassembled 2cm Flak 30 receives attention from a weapons specialist. (PW)

Above: The Plattform-Abschluss AS 5237 mounted at the front of the platform had Seilrolle (cable pulleys) on both sides, which served to haul the 2cm Flak 30 on and off the Sfl. The Sd.Ah.51 (special trailer) is carrying an ammunition box. It could also be used to carry the 2cm Flak 30. (Bundesarchiv Bild 101I-63-2185-27a)

Below: The Selbstfahrlafette (Sd.Kfz.10/4) were issued to both Wehrmacht and Luftwaffe units. (PW)

Above: A Selbstfahrlafette without gun but with brackets for the loading ramps and rifle racks. Originally, each Fla-Kompanie (mot S) had one in three Sd.Kfz.10/4 without a weapon to transport munitions and act as reserve vehicles. (HLD)
Below: A 1939 Selbstfahrlafette (Sd.Kfz.10/4). The 2cm Flak 30 barrel has been removed and stored, and the gun shrouded. Six of the seven-man crew have been photographed by their colleague. (PW)

Reflexvisiere so that they are no longer usable. The Rechendose is inadequate for the high speeds of modern aircraft. Due to the high aircraft speeds and the loss of personnel trained to use the E-Messer (rangefinder), it is usually not used.

The Bereitschaftskasten (ready bins) for magazines mounted on the outside of the vehicle get bent, so that the magazines cannot be pulled out. Sometimes the bins are torn off and lost.

The Bodenwanne (hull) of the 1t Zgkw. gets torn out. This is due to the vehicle being overloaded and over-stressed in pulling the Sonderanhänger 51 with the B-Kasten (bin) mounted. The bin on the trailer is unusable. It interferes with operational readiness because the trailer must be uncoupled when firing. Then it is frequently left behind and often cannot be retrieved. The chassis of the Sd.Ah.51 is too weak.

Because flanking fire is frequently encountered, Panzerschutz (armour protection) on the sides is desired.

The heavier 3t Zugmaschine is proposed as a Sfl. in which the weapon is mounted lower, has a corresponding increase in stowed ammunition, and has better Panzerschutz.

2cm Flak 38. The weapon itself is good, but it is only conditionally usable due to the many gun barrel swellings and bursts in which the cause has not been corrected. There is a continuous shortage of usable reserve gun barrels.

Based on information from the 1.Kp./Fla-Abt.612, most of the burst barrels result from 122 gram ammunition and fewer

with 112 gram ammunition but short bursts occur 1 to 2 metres in front of the gun. There are practically no burst barrels with 120 gram ammunition.

Based on information from the 3.Kp./Fla-Abt.617, there are fewer burst barrels than swollen barrels, which occur 3 to 5cm in front of the chamber. Their cause has been traced back to small flakes being sheared off the driving bands during loading, which get deposited 3 to 5cm in front of the chamber. After 30 to 40 rounds are fired, these deposits lead to the barrel swelling at this location and a stoppage when the barrel gets stuck in the guide sleeve. This never occurs with the 2cm Flak 30.

Once, during loading old Pzgr. ammunition, a preliminary burst occurred that destroyed the breech block and led to the death of crew members in the 1.Kp./Fla-Abt.612. Loading problems continuously occur with the new Pzgr. ammunition. A delivery of Pzgr. alter Art in normal packing arrived at the troops with the Pzgr. loose in the cartridges.

The E.Visiere (range sights) are not usable in Africa because they do not work at all at temperatures exceeding 70°C. The E.Visiere no longer work and are no longer required.

The crews prefer to use the Linealvisier (linear sight), which however is reputed to have a lower chance of getting hits. Due to the lack of a good gun sight, a disadvantage has been found with the 2cm Flak 38 because the gunner sits on the side, instead of behind the gun as on the 2cm Flak 30. This is especially disadvantageous during night firing. The gunner can follow the tracers better when he is directly behind the gun.

A 1940-version Sd.Kfz.10/4 issued as a Munitionsfahrzeug without the 2cm Flak 30. (TA)

Above: A Luftwaffe Selbstfahrlafette (Sd.Kfz.10/4) assembled in 1941 is refitted with a 2cm Flak 38 normally mounted on the wider platform of the Sd.Kfz.10/5. This vehicle is towing a Sonderanhänger 51, on which is mounted a B-Kasten (ammunition and accessories box). Alternatively, the Sd.Ah.51 could be used to carry the 2cm Flak 38 for towing. Photographic evidence shows that the 2cm Flak 30 was also mounted on the wide platform of the Sd.Kfz.10/5. (Bundesarchiv Bild 1011-20-1293-6)

Below: A Waffen-SS 2cm Flak 38 mounted on a Selbstfahrlafette (Sd.Kfz.10/4) (mit Auffahrschienen) and the narrow platform designed for the 2cm Flak 30. (Bundesarchiv Bild 101I-639-4272-37a)

Above: Firing at ground targets, this 2cm Flak 38 with a Schutzschild (armoured shield) is mounted on a Selbstfahrlafette (Sd.Kfz.10/5) with the wider platform designed for the 2cm Flak 38. The gunner is using the Z.F.3x8° Flak direct fire sight. For anti-aircraft fire, the gun was fitted with a Schwebekreisvisier 38. A large Hülsensack (bag to catch spent cartridge casing) was attached on the right side. (Bundesarchiv Bild 101I-298-1768-13)

Below: Selbstfahrlafette (Sd.Kfz.10/5) with the wider platform for a 2cm Flak 38, as completed by M.W.C. in 1943. Despite the date, it still has Fahrtrichtungsanzeiger (turn signals). (HLD)

Above: A 2cm Flak 30 with an armoured shield mounted on a Selbstfahrlafette (Sd.Kfz.10/4) that was issued to Fla-Abt. (Sfl.) 606, which was sent to Libya with the 5.lei.Div. in 1941. (YK)
Below: A Selbstfahrlafette (Sd.Kfz.10/5) with a 2cm Flak 38 (completed by M.W.C. after March 1943) can be identified by no longer having Fahrtrichtungsanzeiger (turn signals). (Bundesarchiv Bild 101I-711-406-7a)

Above: A Selbstfahrlafette (Sd.Kfz.10/5) für 2cm Flak 38 with the wider fold-down platforms. The 2cm Flak 38 is fitted with the Flakvisier 38/40 sighting device for anti-aircraft use and a Z.F.3x8° Flak for direct fire. (PW)
Below: Two Selbstfahrlafette (Sd.Kfz.10/4) but mounting 2cm Flak 38 operating in the east in July 1942. (PW)

Above: This Selbstfahrlafette (Sd.Kfz.10/4) with a 2cm Flak 30 issued to a Luftwaffe unit has been backfitted in 1943 with Behelfspanzerung (expedient armour) to protect the driver, co-driver, and radiator. (Bundesarchiv Bild 101I-455-6-24)
Below: The 8mm thick Behelfspanzerung was also backfitted in 1943 to Selbstfahrlafette (Sd.Kfz.10/5) für 2cm Flak 38 with the wider platforms. (Bundesarchiv Bild 101I-463-351-4)

12. Pak Conversions

Other than photographs, no documentary evidence has been located to date about the practice of makeshift mounting of antitank guns on the le.Zgkw.1t.

By 1 September 1939, a total of 11,200 3.7cm Pak were listed in the inventory of the German forces. A further 6,669 were manufactured, with the last in March 1942, but mass production had effectively ceased in October 1941 with only 35 thereafter.

Chapter 7.2 lists the various K.St.N., for the units authorised to have le.Zgkw.1t for towing the 3.7cm Pak.

A few photographs show that as early as May 1940, during the campaign in France and Belgium, a few units increased the mobility of their 3.7cm Pak by mounting these on top of their le.Zgkw.1t. A 3.7cm Pak in Feuerstellung (firing order) still weighed 450 kg, with the result that such a load could have been detrimental to the reliability of the le.Zgkw.1t in the long term. The photographs show wooden beams were attached to the track guards with further construction that allowed the wheeled 3.7cm Pak to be carried in such a way as to easily be removed without any permanent damage to either the gun or the Zugkraftwagen.

On 19 November 1940, new K.St.N. were published that included the number of 5cm Pak 38 and 3.7cm Pak authorised to be towed by units equipped with the le.Zgkw.1t.

This le.Zgkw.1t assembled by Adler was converted to carry a 3.7cm Pak with its trails in place. The anti-tank gun is mounted on top of the storage bin behind the driver. One of the disadvantages of such makeshift solutions can be seen in that the windscreen has had to be removed, making the task of the driver more unpleasant. The markings show it belonged to the 7.Panzer-Division. (NARA)

A few makeshift Selbstfahrlafette with 3.7cm Pak auf le.Zgkw.1t appeared during the campaign in Yugoslavia. These had more significant long-term changes, such as the removal of the lateral stowage bin behind the driver.

With the invasion of Russia, there is increased evidence of the practice of mounting of Pak on le.Zgkw.1t. but how this was done depended on the unit. In many cases, the 3.7cm Pak Unterlafette (lower carriage) was fixed to the central bin by metal straps bolted to its front and rear; however, since a 3.7cm Pak with wheels was too narrow to fit over the central bin, the wheels had to be removed. The gun trails were often removed; however, the 13.Panzer-Division fastened wooden beams to the track guards that extended to the rear and provided a brace for gun trails.

Some examples featured wooden structures that raised the 3.7cm Pak so that the driver's windscreen could continue to be used in a raised position. Over time, various forms of makeshift armour protecting the radiator and driver were added.

The 5cm Pak 38 weighed 930 kg in Feuerstellung. When carried on the vehicle along with ammunition, it would have overtaxed it. However, the advantage of mobility clearly must have led to any reliability problems being ignored.

The methods of mounting the 5cm Pak 38 mimicked those for the 3.7cm Pak. The mounting had to be higher, since the Oberlafette (upper carriage) of the 5cm was considerably deeper than that of the 3.7cm. Wooden beams were bolted to the fenders with further blocks to hold the axle stubs. The trails of a 5cm were too long for the vehicle. In many cases, these were replaced by steel girders.

The crews operating these makeshift Pak Sfl. were more exposed with their guns at an elevated height. As a result, one can observe the increasing addition of makeshift armour, especially protecting the driver and the radiator.

Considerable ingenuity was used to create this makeshift 3.7cm Pak conversion. (Bundesarchiv Bild 101I-188-345-39-5)

Above: Considerable thought and effort has gone into the construction of the armour on the 3.7cm Pak conversion that was operated by the 216.Infantrie-Division near Smolensk. (TA)
Below: This 5cm Pak38 conversion included a travel lock. (Bundesarchiv Bild 101I-286)

Column of SS troop with their le.Zgkw.1t converted to makeshift Selbstfahrlafette for 5cm Pak 38. The armour was created from whatever was available, resulting in many variations of application. (PW & MZ)

Leichter Zugkraftwagen 1to (Sd.Kfz.10) Ausf.A & B
D 7 Fahrgestell. Fgst.Nr.Serie 100001 - 703500

Measurements

Length, overall	4.75m (**Sd.Kfz.10/4** 5.35m)
Width, overall	1.93m (**Sd.Kfz.10/4** 2.03m)
Height, with Seated Crew	1.57m
Wheel Track, Front Wheel	1.63m
Track Centres	1.58m
Track Contact	1.36m
Fuel Capacity	**Two tanks** 60 + 30 litre or
	One tank 115 litre
Crew	Driver and Co-driver
	Sd.Kfz.10 Up to six troops
	Sd.Kfz.10/4 Gun crew of five
Weight, no Equipment or Fuel	3400 kg (**Sd.Kfz.10/4** 3980 kg)
Combat Weight	4900 kg
Weight on Front Axle	800 kg
Weight on Tracks	4100 kg

Weapons Data

	2cm Flak 30	2cm Flak 38
Muzzle Velocity (115 g HE tracer)	900 m/s	900 m/s
Practical Rate of Fire	120 rpm	180 - 220 rpm
Range	4800m	4800m
Ceiling	3800m	3800m
Elevation	-10° to +90°	-20° to +90°
Traverse	360°	360°
Length, in Firing Order	3.315m	-
Width, in Firing Order	1.285m	-
Height, in Firing Order	1.14m	-
Weight, Stowage Boxes Empty	245 kg	412 kg
Stowage Boxes Loaded	770 kg	750 kg
Length, carried on Sd.Ah.51 Trailer	2.80m	-
Firing Height	0.74m	0.76m
On Sd.Ah.51 Trailer	1.08m	1.12m
Total Weight of Schutzschild	112 kg	120 kg
Gunsight	Flakvisier 35 or Linealvisier 21	

Automotive Capabilities

Maximum Speed	65 km/hr
Normal Road Speed	45 km/hr
Range on Road	260 km with 115l fuel tank
	220 km with 60 + 30l fuel tanks
Cross Country	150 km
Grade on Sand with Towed Load	12°
Without Towed Load	24°
Fording Depth	0.70m
Ground Clearance	0.325m
Ground Pressure	9 kg/cm²
Power Ratio	21.3 HP/ton
Towing Capability	1000 kg

Automotive Components

Engine	Maybach NL 38 TRKM 6 cyl. water-cooled, 3.791 litre petrol. Later HL 42 TRKM 4.198 litre
Power	90, later 100 HP @2800 rpm
Transmission	Maybach VG 102 128 H preselector
1st Gear	5.5 km/hr (F&R)
2nd Gear	9 km/hr (F&R)
3rd Gear	13 km/hr (F&R)
4th Gear	20 km/hr
5th Gear	31 km/hr
6th Gear	48 km/hr @2800 rpm
7th Gear	65 km/hr @2400 rpm
Reverse	1st Gear to 3rd Gear
Steering	Front wheels & differential
Front Tyres	6.00-20 Luka
Suspension, Front Wheels	Transverse leaf spring
Suspension, Tracks	Torsion bar
Drive	Front sprocket
Roadwheels	5x2 per side, 550 mm dia.
Track	Zgw 51/240/160 Zpw 51/240/160 later

This 80-page book looks at the leichter Zugkraftwagen 1t (Sd.Kfz.10) Ausf.A & B. It is illustrated with 14 pages of 1:35 scale CAD drawings by Hilary Doyle and 86 black and white photographs selected for their clarity of detail and rarity of model.

The Panzer Tracts series includes data on more than 350 German armoured vehicles from 1925 to 1945. The development history, unique characteristics, significant modifications, data sheets and armour specifications are solely based on original documents and surviving vehicles.

ISBN 978-1-915969-30-9

Panzer Tracts is an imprint of Panzerwrecks Ltd   www.panzertracts.com

PANZER TRACTS No.9-3
Jagdpanther
Pz.Jgr. Panther (8.8cm) (Sd.Kfz.173)

Hilary Louis Doyle
& Thomas L. Jentz

Featuring 44 pages of accurate multi-view CAD drawings of the Panzerjäger Panther (8.8cm) (Sd.Kfz.173) G1 and G2 based on detailed measurement of surviving vehicles.

Contents

Panzer Tracts is an imprint of:

Panzerwrecks Limited
Great Priors, Church Street
Old Heathfield, TN21 9AH
United Kingdom
www.panzertracts.com

Front cover: One of the initial Jagdpanther after issue to the s.Panzerjäger Abteilung 654 in April 1944 during driver training. (BA)

Rear cover: The recessed rim Geschütznische (gun recess) shows that this Jagdpanther was assembled in the period August to September 1944. Crew members pose for the cameraman while balancing on the 8.8cm gun. (KHM)

Since Panzer Tracts No.9-3 was originally published in 2005 we have improved the quality of the photographs available and reorganised the layout so that all drawings are in one place.

Being based on primary sources, the historical content remains as valid as in 2005; however, there has been progress on minor details that are now included in the drawings. For example, implementing the order to convert from the rubber Antennenfuss to Stahlblech Antennenfuss (steel spring antenna base) was achieved at least at M.N.H. As a temporary solution, shields to protect the air intakes and outlets of the engine compartment were authorised for unit fitting in an H.T.V.Bl. These were installed on at least 15 M.I.A.G assembled Jagdpanther.

Even after 18 years of research, confirmation is still required for the Fahrgestell Nr. Band (chassis numbers) used by M.B.A. Potsdam, the third plant to assemble the Jagdpanther.

The scale drawings in this book were drawn at full scale using a CAD program and printed at 1:10, 1:20, and 1:35 scale. Eight surviving Jagdpanthers were measured in detail to produce these highly accurate as-built drawings within the tolerances allowed to the original assembly firms.

Thanks are especially due to Karlheinz Münch, Lee Archer and Dan Ballou for providing copies of rare and unique photos. Photos were also obtained from the Bundesarchiv-Bildarchiv (BA) and Militärarchiv (BAMA), The Tank Museum (TTM), Archives Départementales de l'Oise (ADO), Stadtarchiv Lünen (SAL), Library and Archives of Canada (LAC), US Army Ordnance Museum (APG), US Heritage and Education Center (USAHEC) and US National Archives (NARA).

Special thanks also go to Al, David, Ed, Frank, John, Mike, Paul and Rob for supporting our efforts in measuring details on surviving Jagdpanthers to create accurate as-built drawings.